WHY IT WORKS !

Maureen Pisani Ph.D.

Why it Works!
Maureen Pisani Ph.D.
www.ProThriveSBH.com

1

HOW THE

"PISANI METHOD"

ENCOMPASSES

TRANSFORMATION &

SUCCESS.

Why it Works!
Maureen Pisani Ph.D.
www.ProThriveSBH.com

UNDERSTANDING WHY HYPNOTHERAPY WORKS

AND

HOW TO CREATE CONSISTENT RESULTS

Why it Works!
Maureen Pisani Ph.D.
www.ProThriveSBH.com

3

COPYRIGHT

CONTENTS

What can Hypnotherapy help with?   7

Chapter 1 –
Introduction   8

Chapter 2 –
Stress – Theory of Mind and Stress   13

Chapter 3
Survival Mechanisms   22

Chapter 4
Self-Identity   34

Chapter 5 –
How Self-Identity Affects Survival Mechanisms 42
- Self-Confidence   43
- Self-Esteem   61
- Self-Acceptance   78
- Self-Worth   96
- Self-Respect   114
- Self-Love   131

Chapter 6 –
How does one re-set to SAFE?   148
- Control your response   153
- Say 5 Big number out of sequence   155
- Ask for a tight hug   156
- Stop, breathe in and Exhale forcefully   158
- Eat Protein every 3 hours   159
- The Bowenwork reset to safe   163

Chapter 7 –
- How does Hypnotherapy Help?   166
- How to release past traumas   167
- How to re-set to safe – hypnotically   171
- How to predetermine behaviors   175
- How to override old triggers   179
- How to introduce self-forgiveness   184
- How to build all the Self-Identity Attributes 191
- How to ensure that new behaviors
  are installed and implemented   212

Chapter 8
Statistics and Statistical Analysis   230

Chapter 9
Personal Observations   238

Chapter 10 –
Conclusion   263

Biography   266

Books   268

MP3s   270

Testimonials   272

Why it Works!
Maureen Pisani Ph.D.
www.ProThriveSBH.com

WHAT CAN HYPNOTHERAPY HELP WITH ?

This modality, initially hailed as merely mesmerizing, is beneficial *holistically,*

It helps work and life thrive *harmoniously,*

Hypnotherapy takes one from looking at life hungrily to living it *heartily,*

It bridges one from being sad and down to living life *happily,*

It dissipates insomnia, so enjoying a great night's sleep every night happens *harmoniously,*

It helps by reducing sickness and upgrading to a body that's *healthy,*

Hypnotherapy can help one re-focus, re-center, and re-set, *hourly,*

It turns sporadic success to a life where one accrues achievements *habitually,*

It facilitates releasing abusive scenarios, and introduces being treated *honorably,*

It converts debilitating scenarios to situations where one wins in life *heroically,*

My wish is that *Hypnotherapy* will be historically known to have been helpful to all *humanity.*

Why it Works!
Maureen Pisani Ph.D.
www.ProThriveSBH.com

7

CHAPTER 1

INTRODUCTION

I've been asked why I became a Hypnotherapist, countless times. My instinctive response is "Because it works!" It sure does. Many lifetimes ago, when I worked in a medical office as a Medical Historian, I got injured. I was diagnosed with bilateral Cubital Tunnel Syndrome and Overuse Syndrome. I ended up undergoing 10 surgeries, 5 on each elbow. This situation lasted for a horrendous six years. Everything that could go wrong, did. I was in constant intense pain, was taking 24 pills a day (14 of which were pain medications), lost 80% grip strength on the right hand and 75% grip strength on the left hand. I could barely function. I jumped through every hoop and obeyed every possible recommendation the orthopedists, neurologists, and all the other physicians I was sent to, came up with. At the end, their solution was to declare me 100% disabled, place me on Social Security, offer me a lifetime supply of medication, and wash their hands of me. I was only 33! The medical specialists had run out of options, and for them, that was an adequate conclusion to my story.

It wasn't acceptable for me.

Why it Works!
Maureen Pisani Ph.D.
www.ProThriveSBH.com

Luckily, I stumbled on Hypnosis, was curious enough to go and find out what it could possibly offer me, and in two Hypnotherapy sessions, the pain was resolved! So, can you see why I wholeheartedly believe that Hypnotherapy works? I'm living proof that it does!

I took my Hypnotherapy training course at the Hypnosis Motivation Institute (H.M.I.), the first nationally accredited college of Hypnotherapy. H.M.I. was founded by Dr. John Kappas, Ph.D., in 1968. It was an incredible course that gifted me a second future.

I'm proud to say that I've been in practice for 16 years now, have helped thousands of clients, have authored 17 additional books, created over 20 MP3s, am the only hypnotherapist who has been a director and instructor in two nationally accredited colleges, co-authored a paper through the Neuro-Science Department at UCLA, was the resident Hypnotherapist at the Chopra Center for almost nine years, and between you and me... I'm just getting warmed up!

I love being a Hypnotherapist. It offers me the opportunity to meet amazing individuals who are ready to upgrade their life but have no idea how to go about it.

Why it Works!
Maureen Pisani Ph.D.
www.ProThriveSBH.com

9

Since I received Hypnotherapy as my last resort, I completely understand how clients feel. Most have attempted everything else and gone to everyone else. Then, either because someone they know refers them to me, or they research Hypnotherapists online and find me, I get to meet them and introduce them to the incredible benefits Hypnotherapy has to offer.

I was fortunate enough to learn the Kappasinian Method of Hypnotherapy. Dr. J. Kappas, Ph.D., was a trailblazer in the field. Yes, hypnosis has been around since Anton Mesmer launched "magnetism" in the 18th century, but for most of the time since then, hypnosis survived as Stage Hypnosis.

In the late 1960's Dr. Kappas decided to introduce the therapeutic aspect of Hypnosis to the public, not only as an alternative therapeutic modality but also as a career. It's thanks to Dr. Kappas that there are distinctive levels of status (Hypnotist, Master Hypnotist, and Hypnotherapist) in the Federal Dictionary of Occupational Titles. Dr. Kappas' forward thinking created a legitimate career for thousands.

Apart from teaching how to induce the hypnotic state in clients, H.M.I also taught the Kappasinian Method, which is different from other styles.

Why it Works!
Maureen Pisani Ph.D.
www.ProThriveSBH.com

Dr. Kappas discovered an unknown aspect of how and why hypnosis works – "how clients understand language." He introduced this information in his book *Professional Hypnotism Manual*, where he explained "Physical and Emotional Suggestibility."

Understanding if the client received language literally vs. inferentially gave us hypnotherapists the insight necessary to adapt our language to match the client's preferred choice, thereby making the receiving of hypnotic suggestions more acceptable and therefore easier to implement. It made all the difference in creating a methodology where results were reproducible, thus making hypnotherapy a dependable modality of change.

In the beginning of my career, I promised myself and all my future clients that I would give them my best. However, I couldn't give them my best if I had only scratched the surface of this incredible world of Alternative Modalities, right?

So, I continued studying, learning, and implementing new techniques and creating my own version of them through the nuances, abreactions, and acceptance levels I observed.

Why it Works!
Maureen Pisani Ph.D.
www.ProThriveSBH.com

11

I was aware of how accruing different modalities offered me the flexibility to personalize my approach to each client, actually to each session, each client has ever had with me. Currently, I'm at the Master Levels in Hypnotherapy, Therapeutic Guided Imagery, Reiki, and am a Trainer of Neuro-Linguistic Programming and Hypnotherapy.

As their Hypnotherapist, I'm in the position where I observe my clients. I'm paying attention to what they say, what they don't say, how they say it, what they prioritize, and what they minimize. I'm listening for intonation, watching body language, listening for the pauses, noticing what they discuss with ease and what's tough to talk about, and much more. Over the years, I've noticed that even though the clients had overcome previous hurdles, facing yet another dilemma invariably causes varying levels of stress.

This stress is either obvious and dealt with (albeit mostly with behaviors that aren't always empowering), and at other times, the covert stress shows up as symptoms or behaviors that interrupt, slow down, or even stop the clients from their everyday life.

Why it Works!
Maureen Pisani Ph.D.
www.ProThriveSBH.com

CHAPTER 2

STRESS

What is Stress? If I had to ask a hundred people, I'd receive a hundred different responses. The definition of Stress is *"a state of mental or emotional strain or tension resulting from adverse or very demanding circumstances."* Stress, basically, is anything that we feel that is outside of our capabilities and overwhelms us.

To some, stress might be dealing with paperwork, bills, and balancing a checkbook, but to an accountant, who loves all financial paperwork, stress could be giving a presentation or networking and meeting new people. Stress to a child might be learning their times tables, but stress to another child might be having to participate in their P.E. class. Stress to extroverts could be not receiving the positive acceptance they were expecting, while stress to introverts could be having to host a party where they're fearful of something going wrong which would embarrass them publicly.

Stress is incredibly personal. However, it's a known fact that stress aggravates 98% of diseases.

Why it Works!
Maureen Pisani Ph.D.
www.ProThriveSBH.com

13

If 'Tom' is a borderline diabetic, being continuously stressed might push Tom all the way through to becoming a full-blown diabetic. It's also important to keep in mind that nowadays we're all experiencing a low level of constant stress which we tend to accept as part of our life, so when we admit to being stressed out, that's above all the other constant stress to which we've gotten accustomed.

When we do experience that intense stress, we respond to it physiologically, mentally, and emotionally.

On a physical level, our body has two systems that respond to stress: the SAM and the HPA axis. These are our nervous and endocrine responses to stress.

The SAM Axis stands for Sympathetic Adrenal Medullary Axis, which is known as the fight/flight response. It's our quick response to short term stress. It's a fast triggered response to save our life. The SAM axis triggers what the body needs to do right now, not focus on secondary functions like digestion or creating cells, but to deal with the threat at hand and get us to a safe place.

It begins in the hypothalamus, which sends a message to the brain stem, which then triggers the sympathetic nervous system.

This in turn signals the medulla of the adrenals, which release epinephrine and norepinephrine into the bloodstream.

Why it Works!
Maureen Pisani Ph.D.
www.ProThriveSBH.com

These hormones increase blood pressure and heart rate and redistribute the circulation to the large muscles, diminishing the blood supply to other areas of the body, as its intention is to supply the person's big muscles with as much energy to facilitate escaping the threat and ensuring survival. This is the appropriate response if these people were facing a hungry saber-tooth tiger. However, as mentioned earlier, what we perceive as stress nowadays usually isn't a life-threatening situation.

The repeated triggering of SAM Axis has long-term negative effects that include hypertension, digestive problems, and suppression of the immune system.

The HPA Axis stands for Hypothalamic Pituitary Adrenal Axis. This response also begins in the brain, in the hypothalamus, which then sends a signal to the anterior pituitary, which in turn relays a message to the adrenal cortex, which releases cortisol.

This elevates blood sugar levels to ensure a prolonged response. When the cortisol levels in the blood are high, a message is sent back to the hypothalamus and hippocampus that will shut down the system, through what's known as a negative feedback mechanism.

As all this is occurring, (for some on a regular basis, and for others several times a day), these physical spontaneous responses, which we know are our survival mechanisms, also affect the emotional and mental aspects of who we are.

When our body goes into high alert, as soon as the sympathetic nervous system is triggered,

Why it Works!
Maureen Pisani Ph.D.
www.ProThriveSBH.com

15

we feel on edge, we are apprehensive, we feel unsafe, tense, stressed out, and afraid. Think of how we feel after what could have been a horrible car crash. We are aware that the crash was a close call, and that it didn't happen, but our heart is still pounding in our chest, our hands are still sweaty, our breathing is still shallow and rapid, and our muscles are shaking. And that's considering that nothing happened!

We experience the same response if we're running late and are caught in traffic, if we have a deadline, if we have to face a situation we'd rather not, as we're waiting in the doctor's examination room.

If a person has that physiological reaction several times a day, feeling unsafe, being hypervigilant, feeling nervous, being suspicious of everything and everyone, it becomes their normal functioning status. That leads to that individual feeling like the world is against them, that something bad is about to happen, and emotionally, they end up scared, worried, negative, pessimistic, unmotivated, and withdrawn.

As all this is occurring, this person's emotions end up affecting their mental perspective. If this individual is living life from this point of view, they are using a tremendous amount of their mental bandwidth filtering and processing life from this negative outlook.

Mentally, they'll be suspicious of everything and everyone, they will be disheartened, will self-doubt constantly, will self-sabotage continuously and feel like they are incapable of handling regular life.

Why it Works!
Maureen Pisani Ph.D.
www.ProThriveSBH.com

The combination of all three aspects creates an individual who is stressed on all levels, feels horrible, is constantly waiting for the next shoe to drop, for the next tragedy to occur, and totally believes that they cannot deal with life. This is where people experience all levels of anxiety.

The constant re-triggering of their sympathetic nervous system wears out all of their reservoirs of resilience, leaving them on empty, without resources, and exhausted.

THEORY OF MIND & STRESS

The Kappasinian Method of Hypnotherapy explains how the Conscious and the Unconscious Minds function through the "Theory of Mind." This theory explains how each of us enters the world with a functioning "Primitive Mind," which has two fears – the fear of loud noise and the fear of falling. The Primitive Mind is also where our Survival Mechanisms reside.

In the first eight years of life, we build our "Unconscious Mind," which is a library of all our known experiences. These experiences set the foundation for how we will function throughout our life. According to what these known experiences are and how we classified them (positive or negative), we identify, associate, and respond to every single stimulus that we face daily.

Why it Works!
Maureen Pisani Ph.D.
www.ProThriveSBH.com

17

Around 9/10/11 years of age, we build our "Critical Mind," a filter that determines what's allowed into the Unconscious Mind.

Around 12/13 years of age, we build our "Conscious Mind," where we have Reasoning, Analyzing Abilities, Decision Making Abilities, a Voice, and Will Power.

When life is going smoothly, our conscious mind is setting goals, thinking of what the next accomplishment is going to be. However, we will only achieve our goals if they are in alignment with what our unconscious mind has determined is acceptable.

According to the Kappasinian Method, the Unconscious Mind is 88% of our mental capability, while the Conscious Mind is 12%. The Unconscious Mind is where the parameters of what we've come to believe is acceptable, safe, or appropriate for us, are located. Unfortunately, if the conscious mind sets a goal that's out of alignment with what the unconscious mind's parameters are, we will not achieve our goal.

The unconscious mind feels safe dealing with repeated known experiences or experiences that are incredibly similar to what we have gotten accustomed to. That's the key. The irony here is that the unconscious mind has only one goal – to keep you safe.

Why it Works!
Maureen Pisani Ph.D.
www.ProThriveSBH.com

The unconscious mind dislikes "unknowns." It is terrified of unknowns, because it cannot gauge if the unknowns are going to be safe for you. The safest approach the unconscious mind has to these unknown situations is to refuse to accept or implement them, thereby making sure that you stay well within your comfort zone.

I've come to realize that what we achieve or fail at is all determined by an Unconscious Homeostasis, which basically means, the need to stay the same.

If "Jane" has been earning $50,000 a year, but she's setting a goal to earn $200,000 next year, Jane won't earn $200,000 because her unconscious mind is accustomed to earning $50,000, which is what it deems safe and acceptable. Jane has an unconscious financial comfort zone that was set by how much her family earned while she was growing up. If they made $50,000, that's what Jane's unconscious mind has set as acceptable and therefore, that's what she earns.

However, when Jane utilizes hypnotherapy and upgrades her unconscious financial comfort zone to $200,000, where suggestions are given as to how safe earning that income will be for her, then she will be able to earn that income. As soon as her unconscious and conscious minds are in alignment, Jane will have 100% of her mental capability working towards the same goal.

Why it Works!
Maureen Pisani Ph.D.
www.ProThriveSBH.com

19

This "Theory of Mind" model not only demonstrates how the unconscious mind is running the show, but also how all levels of function and behavior are affected by how stressed the individual is.

When we get stressed out, we stop functioning from our Conscious Mind, which correlates to the Pre-Frontal Cortex of our brain, also known as the "Adult Brain." We drop straight down to our Primitive Mind, which correlates to our "Reptilian Brain," which is the oldest part of the brain, evolutionarily speaking.

As soon as we drop into our Primitive Mind, our adult reasoning capabilities are gone and we're left with our Survival Mechanisms, or as they are commonly known, "Fight/Flight." These survival mechanisms are our instinctive, prehistoric knee-jerk reactions to life. Remember, our physical body has no idea that we're living in the 21st century.

Physiologically speaking, our bodies react to rush hour traffic stress in the exact same way our prehistoric ancestors reacted to facing a hungry saber-tooth tiger. Our bodies trigger the same adrenaline and cortisol when we're sitting at home juggling the household's finances as our prehistoric ancestors reacted to being attacked by rival villagers.

Why it Works!
Maureen Pisani Ph.D.
www.ProThriveSBH.com

Physiologically speaking, our bodies react to our day-to-day stressors with the same intensity as if we were facing a life-threatening experience.

That's when things spin out on a tangent. That's when behaviors are shocking, when road-rage occurs, when detrimental decisions are made, when unwise food choices are made, because we're not thinking, we're reacting. AND... we're reacting to what we feel is a life-threatening situation, or at least, that's what our Primitive Mind is responding to.

Due to the astronomical levels of stress that each of us is experiencing, this 'spinning out' happens much more frequently than any of us would like to admit.

At some point, when the situation has either reduced in intensity to make it approachable for us, or we have removed ourselves from the threat, we each find a moment where we come to our full awareness and are shocked with what we said, how we said it, what we did, what we bought, what we ate, etc.

During the time when we were in high-stress mode, everything we did seemed reasonable. However, afterwards, once we rise and once again function from our conscious mind, we are appalled at how we handled ourselves and/or the situation.

Stress and how we react to the stressor in the moment of crisis isn't the whole story.

Why it Works!
Maureen Pisani Ph.D.
www.ProThriveSBH.com

21

Over the years, having worked with thousands of clients, I saw them happy, sad, mad, depressed, grieving, livid, unmotivated, incredibly motivated, and every stage in between. I noticed that there was something else that was affecting their resultant behavior, the outcome they called their life.

Yes, stress was triggering most of the behavior, but their Self-Identity levels were either tempering or compounding these survival mechanism responses.

Why it Works!
Maureen Pisani Ph.D.
www.ProThriveSBH.com

CHAPTER 3

SURVIVAL MECHANISMS

The official definition of "survival mechanisms" by Collins Dictionary is *"something you or your body does automatically, in order to survive in a dangerous or unpleasant situation."*

There are five survival mechanisms – Fight, Flight, Freeze, Food, and F^*k (which I have renamed *"The Other F"*).

[I appreciate that adults are reading this book, but if I had to use the F word each and every time, I mentioned that survival mechanism, it would really taint the book's standard. You and I both know what we're referring to, so each time you read *The Other F*, the meaning will not be lost on you. I truly appreciate your understanding me on this.]

I am going to explain each individual survival mechanism so we can all have the same foundation. Over the years, I've learned that assuming that we're both discussing the same topic from the same level of understanding has led to horrific misunderstandings. Therefore, here's a brief description of each of the survival mechanisms we have at our disposal.

Why it Works!
Maureen Pisani Ph.D.
www.ProThriveSBH.com

23

FIGHT – This behavior is when our unconscious mind chooses "action." Fight might be physically hitting someone, however, that is not always the case. Fight is to take action, confront your "attacker," and do something about it.

Reacting to Fight might show up as a bystander witnessing a car crash and running toward the vehicles to help the injured in the cars, running into the middle of a physical altercation to separate the two who are throwing punches, writing a letter to report a wrongdoing, making a call to report an abusive situation, or it might be finally speaking up for oneself after years of being taken for granted or abused.

FLIGHT – This behavior is when our unconscious mind chooses "to escape the scenario." It's not a thought-out process, it just happens, and it's instinctive.

Reacting to Flight might be that one literally runs away from bullies or abusers, but it might also show up as sleeping for 14/18 hours a day, in order not to face the reality of one's life. Flight could also exhibit as deflection – when one does everything else possible instead of that one important thing that needs to get done.

Why it Works!
Maureen Pisani Ph.D.
www.ProThriveSBH.com

FREEZE – This behavior is when our unconscious mind launches an eons' old response to just "Freeze" and become immobile. There are some schools of thought that say that the physical body is prehistoric and that it (as an organism) doesn't realize we're living in the 21st century and freezes as a response that worked for our ancestors. Behaviors that saved the species got transmitted down to the offspring.

Freeze might show up as someone witnessing an accident and being completely unable to move. One might feel frozen in that the intensity of fear triggered in that person literally causes them to shut down. It doesn't have to be a situation when one sees someone else getting hurt. It could also be that they themselves are being attacked and they just stop moving. [I personally witnessed a situation when in a self-defense class, the instructor had choreographed a pretend attack and the young lady chosen for this fell to the floor, landed on her stomach, stiffened like a board, and never fought back. Her defense against being attacked was to freeze.] Freeze can also show up as knowing that an injustice is being done and not speaking up.

Why it Works!
Maureen Pisani Ph.D.
www.ProThriveSBH.com

25

FOOD – This behavior is when our unconscious mind, when facing a threat, chooses to eat first. It's not even that its intention is to nourish the physical body first, but just to eat.

This survival mechanism is launched because the unconscious mind is focusing on ensuring that the physical body has enough fuel to survive to the next day. Think back to prehistoric times. Food supplies weren't guaranteed, so the fear of dying from starvation was real. To eat, during those times, literally meant to continue to be alive. However, nowadays, once in crisis mode, some revert to that behavior.

The Food behavior might show up as binge eating, or it might show up as choosing the high-carbohydrates and high-sugar foods that are known as comfort foods.

When you think about that, comfort foods were initially eaten because they made the person feel better, right? The intake of high carbohydrates will spike the blood sugar levels, which will be perceived by the physical body as a soothing, calming feeling.

Why it Works!
Maureen Pisani Ph.D.
www.ProThriveSBH.com

When someone is in crisis mode and the unconscious survival mechanism of Food is triggered, that individual will disregard everything and anything else and go find food. I can almost guarantee it won't be a protein shake, but items that are high in carbohydrates and sugars. Choosing to eat is not going to solve the crisis, but that individual will feel soothed and on an unconscious level, that person will feel safe knowing that they have enough fuel to survive at least one more day.

'THE OTHER F' – Some refer to this "F" as Fornication, but I'd much rather refer to this as *The Other F* because I prefer to maintain a nonjudgmental approach to this behavior. Fair?

This survival mechanism is triggered when the unconscious mind, while facing a crisis, reverts to prioritizing the continuation of one's bloodline. In the prehistoric era, when life expectancy was about 35 years of age, having children was incredibly important and having grandchildren meant that your genes were what Charles Darwin referred to as "the fittest." *Survival of the fittest* was imperative for our species to thrive.

In a crisis, if one was about to die, one at least knew that his/her children would continue living, so there was continuity of life.

Why it Works!
Maureen Pisani Ph.D.
www.ProThriveSBH.com

27

Considering that today's crises trigger unconscious behaviors stemming from prehistoric times, there are situations when this procreative instinct kicks in. There are times, when having sex for the sake of having sex offers acceptance and satisfies this age-old need for the continuation of a blood line. Yes, this is even triggered when the woman is on birth control. The unconscious survival mechanism overrides all conscious logic and triggers a deep need to find someone to connect with.

This *Other F* survival mechanism is triggered in highly emotional situations, despite who the person is. Afterwards, some feel a variety of negative emotions, including shame, because they cannot compute how when they heard that a loved one had received a terminal diagnosis or got news of a loved one passing away, their instinctive reaction was to have sex. To them, this behavior is inexplicable and usually unacceptable, but it still happens. Explaining this survival mechanism has soothed countless souls.

In his book "Relationship Strategies The E&P Attraction," Dr. Kappas explains how half of the population functions as "Physicals," otherwise known as Extroverts, and how the other half functions as "Emotionals," otherwise known as Introverts.

Why it Works!
Maureen Pisani Ph.D.
www.ProThriveSBH.com

He discusses how they interact, are attracted to each other, and how relationships thrive or crumble because of these traits.

Dr. Kappas also explains how to strengthen and salvage relationships when these traits cause rifts and potential breakups. This behavior is across the board – all genders behave this way to some degree. He explains what triggers extroverts to live the way they do. In his studies, Dr. Kappas found that Extroverts (Physicals) live their life to protect themselves against their greatest fear – Rejection.

So, Extroverts find acceptance of all kinds, but sexual acceptance is what they thrive on in particular. Their need for sex isn't just that they need to satisfy their sexual desire - it's a deep seeded need for the ultimate of acceptance.

Extroverts (Physicals) are usually stressed out the most when there's a rift in a relationship. It's bad if it's a business relationship, but it's horrendous for them if the rift is in their romantic relationship. When extroverts feel the hint of a possible rejection, their instant response is to fix it, remedy it as fast as possible, and bring it back up to the level where the extroverts feel accepted again.

If it is a business situation, usually the extroverts will focus and pay more attention to the person with whom the rift is happening.

Why it Works!
Maureen Pisani Ph.D.
www.ProThriveSBH.com

29

Keeping in mind that for the extroverts, sexual acceptance is the best, so they will approach this situation with intensity. The possibility of being rejected is horrifying for them, so in their mind it is imperative that they resolve it and resolve it now.

Some extroverts might ease their stress by going home and intensifying their sexual frequency with their romantic partners, but others will tackle the problem where the problem lies. They might spend more time with the person at work to see how they can fix the situation.

This might lead to the crossing of ethical boundaries. We have all heard about how professional lines were crossed and "…it just happened…" was the explanation.

According to Dr. Kappas' studies, Introverts (Emotionals) have a completely different wiring. Introverts function from the perspective where they are going to do everything it takes to prevent their greatest fear – The Loss of Control. Introverts will focus on improving their career at all costs. Introverts live their life in their head. They think, strategize, plan, and function with great focus. These introverts have what Dr. Kappas called a "mind-body disconnect," meaning that they do not connect with emotions and feelings but live their life through reason and deduction.

Why it Works!
Maureen Pisani Ph.D.
www.ProThriveSBH.com

Introverts do have sex, but not for the same reasons that extroverts do. Introverts have sex to prevent headaches and stagnation of bodily fluids. (I apologize for the bluntness, but full clarity is essential.) They will have sex with their extrovert partners to soothe the extrovert's insatiable need, because they are aware that if their partner doesn't have sex regularly, emotional situations will escalate between them, and that's exactly what the introverts dislike even more... dealing with the extrovert's gushing emotions, when the introverts have no idea what all the hoopla is about.

Emotions to introverts are annoying, uncomfortable sensations that cause them to feel like they are about to lose control, which is their greatest fear. So, introverts shut down emotions incredibly fast to re-establish internal control. This is where the introverts feel safe.

When the introverts are stressed out or are facing a crisis and they have *The Other F* as their survival mechanism, they will have sex with someone from the office or sometimes even with a stranger. The introvert's mind thrives on unpredictability and the excitement of "unwrapping a new present." They also differentiate between love and sex.

Why it Works!
Maureen Pisani Ph.D.
www.ProThriveSBH.com

31

Extroverts think of love and sex as an intertwined concept – they have sex, so they love the person/ they love the person, so they have sex. Introverts, however, look at love and sex as two individualized concepts. The introverts can love their romantic partner and have sex with their work colleague because the colleague is mysterious, understands their dedication to work and career, and can talk shop afterwards. Sex for the introverts is a means to an end – release and relaxation. The introverts will only experience the full body involvement in life during the few moments of orgasm. The intensity of the release overwhelms the introvert, who is incredibly grateful to return to their mind-controlled approach to living, a few minutes later.

When stressed however, introverts will usually push away sex because their focus is on fixing the problem, which usually involves their career.

If there's a crisis in the company, or there's a deadline coming up (for example, April 15th for tax accountants), their stress level is through the roof. The first priority for the introvert is to get the crisis under control. Once it is under control, and the introverts themselves feel back in control, then and only then will they think of sex with others.

Why it Works!
Maureen Pisani Ph.D.
www.ProThriveSBH.com

If the stress continues to escalate, the introverts can revert to masturbation as a temporary release solution. Introverts pull long hours at work and will dedicate all their energy to their career and to resolving the stressor. This means leaving early and coming home late, usually past their partners' bedtime. Masturbation is an efficient and effective way to relax that doesn't require much planning. As soon as the introverts receive that oxytocin hit that floods their body after orgasm, they're ready to continue working.

Why it Works!
Maureen Pisani Ph.D.
www.ProThriveSBH.com

33

CHAPTER 4

SELF-IDENTITY

What is our Self-Identity? What are the components that make up Self-Identity?

Self-Identity is that instinctive acknowledgement of who I am, what my strengths and weaknesses are, what I like and dislike, who I love and what I hate and why, what I can or cannot do, what I deserve or don't, how I evolve in life, how I live my life, what I do, what I think about, how I think about it, what I feel and all the other characteristics that make me who I am.

Self-Identity is made up of Self-Confidence, Self-Esteem, Self-Acceptance, Self-Worth, Self-Respect, and Self-Love. When each of these attributes are strongly positive, we feel incredible. However, if one or more of these attributes is low or negative, then our response to life and how we experience life will tend to be bumpy.

Here's a brief description of what each attribute is, how it originates and what events or incidents improve it or reduce it.

Why it Works!
Maureen Pisani Ph.D.
www.ProThriveSBH.com

SELF-CONFIDENCE

The definition of Self-Confidence is *"trust in one's abilities, capacities and judgment."*

Self-Confidence is the ability to know that "Yes, I can" feeling internally. Self-Confidence is built and strengthened with each activity that we've taken on, completed, and accomplished.

Initially, as we're going through the learning stages, we do "it," but we might do it inaccurately or poorly, but when we keep at it, our perseverance keeps finessing how well we do "it" until it becomes an unconscious behavior. As soon as we reach the fourth and final level of learning, where we become unconsciously competent, then we know without a doubt that we can do "it."

We've all done this. When babies are learning how to walk, they all go through the exact same learning process. That's exactly what you and I did when *we* were learning how to walk. We fell on our diapers millions of times, but with each failed attempt, we learned how to shift our weight, how to stand correctly, how to engage which muscle for which movement, which muscle was next, and slowly but surely, we learned how to walk.

Why it Works!
Maureen Pisani Ph.D.
www.ProThriveSBH.com

35

In fact, if anyone asked you today if you know how to walk, you wouldn't hesitate and instantly respond with a solid "Yes." One can conclude that your self-confidence in your ability to walk is high, because walking is second nature to you.

So, whether your self-confidence is high or low depends solely on what you perceive your ability to be regarding how well you can do "_____." Ironically, if you believe that you can do something, you will. However, low self-confidence, albeit a mental perspective, reduces our capability and effects the outcome negatively. Remember Henry Ford's quote *"Whether you think you can, or think you can't, you're right."* Well... he was.

SELF-ESTEEM

The definition of Self-Esteem is *"an individual's sense of his/her value or worth, or the extent to which a person values, approves of, appreciates, prizes or likes themselves."*

In our context, Self-Esteem is the measure of what and how much we think we deserve. If I am aware that I deserve a 9 (on a 1-10 scale), but am only given a 7,

Why it Works!
Maureen Pisani Ph.D.
www.ProThriveSBH.com

I'm going to speak up and ask why I wasn't given a 9. In this case, it would be fair to state that I had a high level of self-esteem.

If, however, I have low self-esteem, then internally I would believe that I only deserve a 4, on that 1-10 scale, so whatever is given to me regardless of what it is, I might accept because I truly don't think I deserve anything at all. If a person has high self-esteem and is treated poorly in a relationship, that person will demand to be treated better, and if that better treatment doesn't occur, then that

individual will leave that relationship. However, the person with low self-esteem will be aware that they are being treated poorly but will stay because internally they don't believe they deserve any better.

SELF-ACCEPTANCE

The definition of Self-Acceptance is *"an individual's acceptance of all of his/her attributes, positive or negative."*

Self-Acceptance is fickle. Most mislabel self-acceptance as being conceited, but it isn't. Self-Acceptance is the acknowledgment of knowing who you truly are – the good, the bad, and the ugly.

Why it Works!
Maureen Pisani Ph.D.
www.ProThriveSBH.com

37

There is nothing conceited about knowing that you know what your strengths are, or what your weaknesses are, or what your kneejerk reactions are when you're attacked, cornered, betrayed, or admired, respected, and loved.

Accepting oneself is incredibly liberating. Instead of depending on what people around you have said you are, accepting yourself is allowing for growth and learnings to be absorbed, for maturity and evolving to occur.

Self-acceptance is the deep innate knowing who you truly are from every angle and every perspective. You have full choice to accept who you are currently, while simultaneously knowing that as you live through every experience, you're accruing more learning, which will assist in your evolving, and at which point, you will then accept who you have become.

SELF-WORTH

The definition of Self-Worth is *"the internal sense of being good enough and worthy of love and belonging from others."*

Why it Works!
Maureen Pisani Ph.D.
www.ProThriveSBH.com

Self-Worth is based on how worthy we feel we are, which is derived from what we've been told about how worthy we are. Our unconscious mind builds a library of knowns during the first eight years of our life, also known as the "Imprint years." We build our worth according to how people treated us, what they said to us, and what they gave us. If, during the first 8 years of life, we are given beautiful gifts on a regular basis, told how precious we are and how much we are loved, and treated with love and kindness, then we grow up with high levels of self-worth. However, if our imprint years were years of struggle, abuse, harshness, limitations, and lack, then we grow up with low levels of self-worth.

The level of self-worth determines how we treat ourselves. If I have low levels of self-worth, then I won't really care what choices or decisions I make, because inside I truly believe I'm not worth much. However, if I have high levels of self-worth, then it will matter to me which choices I make and what decisions I take, because I know that I am worthy... worthy of the best!

Why it Works!
Maureen Pisani Ph.D.
www.ProThriveSBH.com

39

SELF-RESPECT

The definition of Self-Respect is *"a feeling of self-worth and self-esteem, a proper regard for one's values, character and dignity."*

Self-Respect is that knowing deep down inside that you value who you are and therefore honor yourself by doing your best and being the best, you can be.

When one has high levels of self-respect, thinking patterns, decisions, choices, and actions are all based according to whether they are in alignment with one's self-worth. However, when one has low levels of self-respect, decisions made don't reflect such care and/or attention. Decisions coming from a low self-respect perspective are destructive and detrimental to oneself and/or others.

SELF-LOVE

The definition of Self-Love is *"a state of appreciation for oneself that grows from actions that support our physical, psychological and spiritual growth. Self-love means having a high regard for your own well-being and happiness."*

Self-Love is the ability to appreciate oneself with full acceptance. Self-love creates the foundation and environment for positive, expansive decisions. When one has high levels of self-love, thinking

Why it Works!
Maureen Pisani Ph.D.
www.ProThriveSBH.com

patterns, choices and decisions are positive, kind, and proactive, which create empowerment.

When one has low levels of self-love, thinking patterns, choices and decisions usually have self-sabotage as a primary bias, which often results in continuous disappointment (even of oneself), and repeated losses and failures.

Why it Works!
Maureen Pisani Ph.D.
www.ProThriveSBH.com

41

CHAPTER 5

HOW SELF-IDENTITY AFFECTS SURVIVAL MECHANISMS

Now, that we have a basic understanding of what our Self-Identity and Survival Mechanisms are, we can start looking at how each of these aspects affects the other.

As we go through each Self-Identity attribute, I will walk you through how high levels and low levels of each will affect each survival mechanism and the resultant behavior that one might observe.

Yes, I will be describing extremes. I will discuss the solid black and brilliant white scenarios, even though I'm fully aware that each of us is living a unique shade of grey from moment to moment. The intention behind being so extreme in my descriptions is to make it easier for you to recognize the behaviors and the possible outcomes.

Most think that we have a primary survival mechanism, and that that's the only one we utilize throughout our lives. In actuality we can access all five, so getting to know the full spectrum of how people respond to crises will be an eye opener.

Why it Works!
Maureen Pisani Ph.D.
www.ProThriveSBH.com

SELF-CONFIDENCE

FIGHT

- High Levels of Self-Confidence and Fight -

This combination of traits creates individuals who know they can and do take action when necessary.

In life, you can see people going after what they wish and desire. Individuals who feel secure about themselves, people who are confident about their traits and capabilities. They function with full strength, living life to the fullest, knowing that they set *and* achieve their goals. They come across as strong, vibrant, a force to be reckoned with. They push forward in life, setting goal after goal, accruing accomplishment after accomplishment with limitless energy, everlasting confidence, knowing that if Plan A doesn't work, they have 25 other plans to test out.

High levels of self-confidence also translate to strong resilience, because these people know that they can, so if they've suffered a setback, they know that they will dust themselves off and relaunch. This comeback attitude is also known as GRIT, and it's been known to be the X factor of success.

Why it Works!
Maureen Pisani Ph.D.
www.ProThriveSBH.com

43

-   Low Levels of Self-Confidence and Fight -

This combination of traits creates individuals who aren't quite sure if they are going to succeed in taking the necessary action, even though every fiber inside them is screaming to go for it. These individuals will talk the big talk but crumble in an instant when it matters. They will have a trigger temper, have anger issues, will live a life overflowing with frustration. These people will have a history of nonstarters (projects that were a great idea but were never begun, let alone implemented or completed), and they will also have a long list of projects that launched but weren't finished. They talk the big talk, but there's usually nothing of substance in what they do.

These individuals see the issue, instinctively feel the need to take action, but in the moment just before they launch into action, there's that doubt that's yelling in their unconscious mind, "do you really believe you can do _____?" which instantly nullifies all the momentum and transforms them into victims.

These people also experience an intense sense of self-loathing because they know how they behave and even though they will continue to use big words, where they exhibit a very loud bark. Unfortunately, that's where it all ends…because there is no bite, and they know it.

Why it Works!
Maureen Pisani Ph.D.
www.ProThriveSBH.com

The male version of this combination is usually also dependent on penile size. Unfortunately, most men evaluate themselves and their capabilities according to the size of their penis.

Most of the male population, globally, live their life, set their goals, and approach romantic relationships based on how confident about their penises they are.

When a man has what he considers a small penis, his self-confidence is usually low. Across time, penile size and sexual prowess have been standards that men have valued immensely. So, knowing that if push came to shove, his penis wouldn't be sufficient to impress, the guy would rather walk away then allow what he considers disappointing evidence to become public.

FLIGHT

- High Levels of Self-Confidence and Flight -

This combination of traits creates individuals who are wired to escape and flee from the situation. They know that they *can* do what is needed, but not during the emergency, or during a high-stress event. The best they can do, is maybe do what is required in the shadows.

So, they will work as an Executive Assistant, backstage, away from the spotlight. They are the dependable IT technicians who keep all systems going... but they are never comfortable being acknowledged for their hard work.

Why it Works!
Maureen Pisani Ph.D.
www.ProThriveSBH.com

45

This combination could also present with personalities and behaviors generally known as "back-seat drivers" or "Monday morning quarterbacks."

They'll comment on what should have been done, and how it should have been handled, but they will never step up to do it *properly* or in the moment when it's needed, themselves.

On one hand they are pushed towards doing whatever needs to be done, because they know they can. On the other hand, they are pushed to flee from the situation. This continuous pushing and pulling in opposite directions can be incredibly frustrating for them.

- Low Levels of Self-Confidence and Flight -

This combination of traits creates individuals who believe they cannot do whatever it is they need to do, and will deflect, procrastinate, and avoid facing that situation at all costs!

This behavior usually stems from one of two general scenarios – (i) either the child had an overly protective parent who did everything for them or (ii) the child was admonished and punished for doing "it" wrong so many times, that the child decided that they just couldn't do "it," or anything else.

Why it Works!
Maureen Pisani Ph.D.
www.ProThriveSBH.com

In the scenario when the parent did most of everything for the child, the parent might believe that they are helping the child, but the child receives the message that the parent is doing "it" for them because the parent doesn't believe that they have the capability to accomplish it.

In the scenario when the parent admonishes and punishes the child for every wrong decision, the parent might be a perfectionist, thereby seeing their child's mistakes as constant

reminders of how imperfect the child is. The more mistakes the child makes, the more upset the parent is, the more admonishing comments are said, and the more mistakes the child makes. It's a losing loop and will only create adults who continuously self-sabotage their life.

We all learn from our mistakes, and usually learning curves are shortened because of the mistakes. Yes, mistakes are essential to learning and upgrading in life. So, when the child isn't allowed to make mistakes, or allowed to even attempt that project, the internal belief will be that they believe that they cannot do "_" (whatever the project might be). As the child grows, that belief overflows into every aspect of life, be it professional or personal.

Why it Works!
Maureen Pisani Ph.D.
www.ProThriveSBH.com

47

This combination of traits creates individuals who are on the outskirts of society, looking in, hoping maybe one day to participate with the regular people, but knowing deep down inside that they don't have the courage to face the people in regular activities or events. If by some chance they should find themselves in an experience, they believe that they would fail horribly at starting or maintaining a conversation, socializing, and/or even interacting with others. The fear of failing publicly will reinforce their fleeing and staying away.

You will notice that I've said that they will believe that they cannot do something. I haven't said that they cannot do something, because the truth of the matter is that they can do anything they desire.

All they have to do is…. Do it! They might be horrible at it in the beginning but giving it a shot will be a start. After all, isn't that how all of us learned how to live life?

FREEZE

- High Levels of Self-Confidence and Freeze -

This combination of traits creates individuals who know what they can do, can produce, can achieve, but are terrified of making the wrong decision, so they freeze and don't do anything.

Why it Works!
Maureen Pisani Ph.D.
www.ProThriveSBH.com

The only way to never make a wrong decision is to never make a decision. So, these people, albeit fully aware of what their capabilities truly are, will never take that step to fulfill their potential.

They will help others succeed, be there for them, help and guide them. These individuals will also help make someone else's company more money. They are the perfect second in command. These people will come up with ideas that they can implement and will, as long as it's for someone else's company, and/or under someone else's name.

If they find themselves in a situation where they need to work in order to advance, then their survival mechanism of FREEZE will kick in, and nothing's completed. Yes, they will do some work, enough to convince everyone else that they are doing what's expected, but in reality, when they come close to the deadline, something will come up to disrupt, derail, or even completely ruin whatever they have been doing.

The ultimate result is that nothing is ever completed, and these people can never reach the success they truly deserve.

Why it Works!
Maureen Pisani Ph.D.
www.ProThriveSBH.com

49

This combination of traits creates individuals who don't believe that they can do anything. In this case, these people will either simply not achieve anything because their actions have to be in alignment with their true beliefs, or they will place themselves in situations that are too difficult or too intricate for them to succeed. These choices will ensure that they will fail at everything they attempt, thereby confirming that they cannot do anything successfully.

These individuals know that they need to earn a living, so they will be employed doing something menial or repetitive. They will work in a field where most of their responsibility is beyond basic. They usually prefer to work at a basic level, and if for some reason the possibility of a promotion becomes available, they will refuse to do what's expected to shine and therefore remove any possibility to be chosen for the promotion.

These people's comfort zone is being in the shadows. Should there be an accident, a crisis, or an incident where something needs to be done quickly, they will freeze. They will be completely unable to move or speak, let alone take action.

Why it Works!
Maureen Pisani Ph.D.
www.ProThriveSBH.com

The panic that arises within them literally stops them from functioning, and once the crisis has been dealt with, they will feel awful and apologize profusely, but truth be told, they were quite aware that they were never going to do anything about it, because they never have.

In the business world, these people will never volunteer to run a project, and are usually quite content to do the grunt work. However, they can only function and complete the grunt work if everything's going smoothly. If anything, negative occurs, or if there's any stress about meeting a deadline, they will freeze, and the more pressure is present, the harder it will be to get them to do anything.

This is also seen in relationships, where one of the partners has goals, plans, and ideas on how to make the relationship, the family, or even the house, better. When these plans are shared, these individuals usually don't object. They will nod in agreement or even go as far as offering a verbal agreement, but they never have any intention of implementing any of the projects the partner is proposing. These individuals believe that they cannot achieve any of the proposed ideas. When the partner's patience starts wearing thin, the more pressure the partner puts on them, the angrier the partner gets, the more frustrated the partner gets, and the more frozen they are in their behavior. This is a disastrous situation for the relationship.

Why it Works!
Maureen Pisani Ph.D.
www.ProThriveSBH.com

51

When these people behave this way in the business world, all that can happen to them is that they might be fired. However, in a relationship, this behavior is not understood and is only seen as defiant, rebellious, or invalidating behavior which, after a while, usually results in the end of that relationship.

FOOD

- High Levels of Self-Confidence and Food -

This combination of traits creates individuals who know what they can do, both in their professional and personal lives. As they go through life, when everything is going smoothly, they will be incredibly productive and successful. They are the go-getters who set and achieve their goals.

When life is going smoothly, these people will have full lives, and usually categorize food as fuel. These people eat to live, not live to eat. They approach eating their meals knowing what the caloric value is, what's good for their body, and why they decided on that choice of food.

However, when a crisis occurs and/or they are stressed out, they then resort to food to calm themselves down. They are aware of how eating food as a soothing mechanism can backfire on their health and weight, so they will indulge by eating massive salads to (i) soothe with food but soothe with awareness and (ii) be fully aware that adding a whole avocado (when ½ is the daily portion) is breaking the rules, but it's still a healthy fat to ingest.

These individuals are fully aware that their decisions on what to eat will always have repercussions, so because they value their capabilities, they won't spin out too much. These people will feel the stress, be triggered, and when that knee jerk reaction of the survival mechanism "Food" kicks in, they are still able to manage what and how much is eaten.

-   Low Levels of Self-Confidence and Food   -

This combination of traits creates individuals who don't believe they can achieve anything. Regardless of what level they are professionally, if there is a learning curve in that profession, they will always feel like the perpetual novice. These people will completely nullify everything that they know about the field in which they work. What they usually focus on are all those new aspects of the profession that they haven't completed learning.

Let's focus on accountants who might function this way. Even though they have been in business for decades, technically they can look back and see the thousands of

Why it Works!
Maureen Pisani Ph.D.
www.ProThriveSBH.com

53

clients they have successfully helped and feel a sense of accomplishment supported by a healthy dose of expertise and wisdom. However, individuals with this combination of traits will ignore those decades of success and focus only on the fact that they haven't learned all the new laws and all their subsequent nuances, by heart, yet.

When these people face a crisis or a trigger that intensifies their stress level, they will resort to eating everything and anything that they think will soothe them to the point where that intense level of stress diminishes.

What these people don't realize is that after gorging or binging on all the wrong choices of food, all they are going to feel is … worse. All that binge eating will absolutely raise their blood sugar level to offer that temporary soothing drowsiness, but after a while as their body starts metabolizing the sugars, that sugar rush ebbs away and within a couple of hours, not only is all that extra ingested sugar gone, but the body has dropped into a low blood sugar level which allows for Adrenaline and Cortisol to be released. These stress hormones amplify whatever mood they are in, so if after all this they are still stressed, these hormones will escalate them to feeling frantic and panicked.

All this will reinforce and solidify their belief that they just cannot accomplish anything.

Why it Works!
Maureen Pisani Ph.D.
www.ProThriveSBH.com

And so, begins that self-fulling prophecy where their thinking patterns go in circles: "I feel bad because I can't do anything, and because I can't do anything I binge on bad foods, which makes me feel bad."

This binging behavior exacerbates irregular blood sugar levels, which intensify irritability, which in turn results in being physiologically stressed out constantly. The blood sugar rollercoasters create cravings for carbohydrates and sugars, and once ingested, the entire loop is triggered again. This leads to a constant level of brain fog, where these individuals feel scatterbrained, unfocused, miserable, and uncertain of who they are and what they can do.

The Other F

- High levels of Self-Confidence & *The Other F*
-

This combination of traits creates people who are sure of themselves, who know how much they produce and achieve.

Why it Works!
Maureen Pisani Ph.D.
www.ProThriveSBH.com

55

They are aware that whatever they put their mind to, they will complete, one way or the other. This high level of self-confidence covers most aspects of their lives, both professionally and personally.

These individuals feel quite certain that if they know something, they can do it. If they don't know something, they know that all they have to do is study and learn it, which will lead to them conquering the topic and achieving their goal.

When the extroverted people are stressed out or are facing a crisis and their survival mechanism is *The Other F*, then these individuals will experience this persistent urge to have sex. If they are in a relationship, then the partner is usually their primary choice. They experience this drive as if they are caught on this runaway train where there is only one outcome – sexual climax and release, which, in reality for these people, means acceptance, relaxation, and safety.

Knowing how the extrovert feels about their other capabilities, these individuals also take pride in their sexual prowess. To them, sex is a sport in which they excel, so when they are stressed out, the urge to copulate is instinctive, urgent, necessary, and undeniable.

Why it Works!
Maureen Pisani Ph.D.
www.ProThriveSBH.com

However, because extroverts have high levels of self-confidence, they will not go for "quickies," because that might reflect badly on their sexual reputation. They are known in every aspect of their life as being exceptionally good at what they do. So, where sex is concerned, the extroverts need to maintain their reputation so that sex for them will be a full body experience, not just a sexual release.

These people will be known amongst close friends as having a strong libido, joking that sex is the best cardio in town. They will always hint that living life to the fullest is truly the secret to staying young.

Even though extroverts enjoy sex on the good days, when they are stressed out there will be more activity with greater intensity because they are fully aware of how incredibly relaxing that rush of oxytocin is. So, they will aim for multiple orgasms in one sexual encounter to release as much stress as possible, and to receive as much oxytocin as possible. They are fully aware of how relaxing that hugging hormone is and know that it's the fastest way to transform their mental/ physical/ emotional status back into relaxed, satisfied, and easy going.

Why it Works!
Maureen Pisani Ph.D.
www.ProThriveSBH.com

57

Introvert people, who are aware of their capabilities to produce and achieve, take it personally when stressed out or facing a crisis, because if they don't succeed in resolving the issue, it's their reputation that's at stake. They will work longer hours and neglect everything and everyone else to focus on resolving the issue. That means that their family, kids, hobbies, friends, and everything else, falls by the wayside.

As these individuals pull all kinds of long hours to work and resolve the problem they are facing, they are still human and stress levels are still felt, so they might resort to masturbation, which is an easy, effective, and efficient system to release the nagging pressure, clear their minds, and feel ready to return to facing and dealing with the problem. They will go to any length to meet the deadline, resolve the issue, and return to their usual normal, calm thinking-through-life disposition.

- Low levels of Self-Confidence & *The Other F* -

This combination of traits creates individuals who are aware that they really don't have what it takes to achieve the goals they set or secretly hope for. People with this perspective present as individuals who will promise the world and disappoint most of the time.

Why it Works!
Maureen Pisani Ph.D.
www.ProThriveSBH.com

They will usually have a reason, a situation that if it hadn't happened, they would have been able to pull through and succeed. They function with an "If only" story. ("If only Covid-19 hadn't happened, I would have become a millionaire. Yup, that's how good my idea was.") Only with these people, it doesn't have to be a global pandemic; it could be rush hour traffic, or simply the fact that for a project to be a success, follow-through, persistence, continuity, and perseverance are necessary to achieve completion.

These individuals know what their track record is, and so they extrapolate that if they haven't succeeded until

now, there's a low probability that they will succeed in the future. This of course is completely unfair to themselves, but that's how they function.

When these people are stressed out or are facing a crisis, let's say they're being pressured to meet a quota, and their survival mechanism is *The Other F*, they know they're not good at accomplishing much, and that their personal track record is at best, mediocre, so when it comes to sex, they usually aren't very good at it either.

Why it Works!
Maureen Pisani Ph.D.
www.ProThriveSBH.com

59

Even though the extroverts feel the desperate need to have sex, because they've been told how they leave a lot to be desired, and how average their sexual performance has been, their desperate need to experience sexual release will trigger them to have "quickies." This is acceptable to them, because performance anxiety reduced to a quickie automatically delineates that the purpose of the encounter is sexual release, not foreplay, intimacy, or connection, but just orgasm.

These extroverts will compound their stress level, because if the coital experience isn't satisfactory, then they judge themselves critically, which will increase the rejection feeling and therefore increase their stress.

The introverts, who know that they're not exactly capable of producing or achieving their goals, when stressed out or facing a crisis, will initially work on resolving the issue, but the more they are incapable of resolving it, the more the desire to have sex builds up. Introverts are looking for the sexual release but are also aware that the more stressed they are, the less likely they will be able to orgasm, which just intensifies the stress.

Why it Works!
Maureen Pisani Ph.D.
www.ProThriveSBH.com

If the introverts are in the vicinity of their extrovert partners, the extroverts will offer to have sex with them, because the extroverts know how relaxing having that sexual release with that flood of oxytocin is, but the introverts will have difficulty climaxing.

Introverts, even if in loving relationships, might choose to masturbate, because this way it's on their terms, and if they cannot achieve orgasm, at least it's their private and confidential situation.

SELF-ESTEEM

FIGHT

- High Levels of Self-Esteem and Fight -

This combination of traits creates individuals who are very aware of what they deserve from the world around them. They know they deserve the best and whenever a situation arises, they will take the necessary action to ensure that they receive the best.

This is a great combination that makes moving upward in one's career and life effortless. These people are wired to take action, so they will do the necessary work to be seen, noticed, and awarded Employee of the Month, or #1 in Sales or whatever the highest standard of success is for them. They will strive towards bigger & better clients, portfolios, positions, and seemingly achieve them with ease.

Why it Works!
Maureen Pisani Ph.D.
www.ProThriveSBH.com

61

However, on a personal level, they might come across as demanding and sometimes even conceited. They will use grandiose complimentary descriptions when they refer to themselves, and seem to feel quite entitled when discussing what's owed to them.

These people walk a fine line, as they decide how much to expose what they believe they deserve vs. what they share publicly.

They are usually go-getters, someone who might be described as a "no nonsense" person. Knowing that these people have a healthy self-identity, they won't accept any stupidity, incompetence, or duplicity. As soon as they recognize that they are not receiving the quality that they know they deserve, that's it. They will disconnect, break away, and will not feel the necessity to explain why. They know that the other part of the conversation / communication / deal was attempting to see how much they could get away with, and they are not going to waste any time on those games.

- Low Levels of Self-Esteem and Fight -

This combination of traits creates individuals who take action but lose momentum whey they're about three-quarters of the way through.

Why it Works!
Maureen Pisani Ph.D.
www.ProThriveSBH.com

These individuals are triggered to respond with the Fight aspect of the survival mechanisms, but because of their low self-esteem, they are unsure of how much they truly deserve, which translates into them not knowing for sure what to accept. This uncertainty covers all aspects of their lives. They will present strong and initially talk the big talk, but as the details of the deal are discussed, they lose the wind out of their sails and agree to, or settle for much less than the going rate, much less than what even they themselves think of as acceptable.

In a relationship setting, these individuals show up strong in the beginning of the relationship, but then will tolerate all kinds of negative behavior, even abusive behavior from their partner because they truly believe that that's all they deserve.

They will be subservient to their romantic partner, they will repeatedly forgive all kinds of insults, snide remarks, being humiliated publicly, and never speak up or even bring up the incidents later, in private.

The low self-esteem levels undermine every instinctive spark of "hey, that's not fair!" or "that was rude" or "I know you're lying," because as soon as they think it, the low self-esteem belief will instantly shut it all down as they think to themselves "I'm lucky this person is still with me! At least I'm still in a relationship!"

Why it Works!
Maureen Pisani Ph.D.
www.ProThriveSBH.com

63

FLIGHT

- High Levels of Self-Esteem and Flight -

This combination of traits creates people who, from one aspect, understand and believe that they deserve the best, but in a crisis or stressful situation, will escape and avoid facing the situation.

These individuals know that they deserve to be treated with respect, but in the moment of truth, they will cower from confrontation and not demand proper treatment. Afterwards, they are usually quite upset with themselves because they know what they should have done/said, but because "Flight" was triggered, all they could do was exit and leave the scene.

This combination results in a lot of internal frustration because these people live two realities – the internal one, when they can visualize and plan what to say to whom when they aren't being treated properly; and the external one, where they shut up, walk away quietly, or simply nod in mute agreement because that's all they can muster in that moment.

Why it Works!
Maureen Pisani Ph.D.
www.ProThriveSBH.com

- Low Levels of Self-Esteem and Flight -

This combination of traits creates people who truly don't believe that they deserve success, and when push comes to shove, in that moment of truth where they can break through and succeed, they walk away. These individuals' behavior might stem from them attempting to do something as a child, but failing at it, so that early in childhood, they decided that they didn't deserve to succeed.

This could have been anything – from not getting the main role in the school play, not making the team, being unable to learn how to ride a bicycle, attempting to cook something and burning it, to attempting to impress the teacher with an assignment but failing horribly… anything.

However, that disappointment became an internal belief that they didn't deserve to "_____" (fill in the blank), because that's how these peoples' unconscious mind works. The lack of deserving ends up overflowing into every aspect of their life.

When these people are facing a situation which they determine is stressful, all this lack of deserving is triggered, reinforced, and compounded with the innate need to disappear.

Why it Works!
Maureen Pisani Ph.D.
www.ProThriveSBH.com

65

These people will make an effort and attempt the project, but the belief that they don't deserve to succeed will sabotage that effort. They will also deflect/avoid/procrastinate to not have to face doing the project.

This behavior usually results in these people having a very low opinion of themselves. To add insult to injury, because of the lack of results or the mediocre results that they have produced, their reputation with others will be mediocre too.

FREEZE

- High Levels of Self-Esteem and Freeze -

This combination of traits creates people who know what they truly deserve, but when something happens that goes against these standards, these individuals will freeze and stay silent. This combination creates a lot of frustration and negative self-talk, because internally they know what's acceptable and what isn't.

These people also know what they need to say or do, but in the moment, they stay silent and simply don't respond or react.

Why it Works!
Maureen Pisani Ph.D.
www.ProThriveSBH.com

Their freezing response could have been triggered in childhood, when maybe they did take action and the repercussions were terribly painful. This lesson caused them to freeze, so this way they can never be blamed for good or bad behavior because their choice to freeze means that they didn't do anything that can be judged.

Unfortunately, in certain situations, not reacting is a response in and of itself, which means that their freezing can still cause them to be judged and they will still experience repercussions, even if in their mind, they believe they didn't do anything.

- Low Levels of Self-Esteem and Freeze -

This combination of traits creates people who believe that they don't deserve anything good. In fact, these individuals will find themselves in situations where the unthinkable happens, and instead of seeing who the culprit/instigator of the bad action was, and react accordingly, they will blame themselves internally for everything and anything that goes wrong, but they will never do or say anything about it.

These people usually have gone through a traumatic event, where instead of realizing how wrong the other

Why it Works!
Maureen Pisani Ph.D.
www.ProThriveSBH.com

67

person was, they took on the blame because they believe that that's how they should be treated. Instead of fighting or reacting in any way, these individuals will simply take it. They will never fight back, and instead will accept that this treatment is just their lot in life.

If the other person in the argument attempts to push these people into a reaction, they will simply freeze more than before. It truly doesn't matter if they would like or dislike the potential outcome, these people simply won't respond. This freezing behavior usually infuriates the other person, which of course creates more stress, which in turn intensifies these individuals' freezing response.

FOOD

- High levels of Self-Esteem and Food –

This combination of traits creates people who are very aware of what they deserve, and function from a perspective that everyone deserves the best in life and should strive to achieve it. When life is going smoothly, they will have healthy boundaries, where their behavior is professional and appropriate.

Why it Works!
Maureen Pisani Ph.D.
www.ProThriveSBH.com

These people will be aware as to where the lines-in-the-sand are for them and will also make decisions that will keep them within the lines of propriety.

When calm, they will choose what to eat very wisely, knowing what they will eat and what the health benefits of their choices are. If these individuals should choose to cheat and stray from their usual wise eating patterns, their choices will still be only mildly bad, because they truly believe that they deserve the best, and that includes best health, too.

However, if these individuals face a crisis or are stressed out, and the survival mechanism Food is triggered, then they will eat larger quantities of the mildly bad foods as comfort foods.

They might choose to eat more cheese or peanut butter late at night because both will soothe, but these people can rationalize that the cheese was seen as protein, while the peanut butter was eaten because of the protein and tryptophan qualities. Yes, they will overindulge, but if these individuals truly spin out, they might eat one candy bar instead of choosing to inhale a dozen doughnuts.

Why it Works!
Maureen Pisani Ph.D.
www.ProThriveSBH.com

69

- Low Levels of Self-Esteem and Food -

This combination of traits creates people who don't believe they deserve anything good or beneficial.

When life is going smoothly, they will function at a low level, just enough to not get fired.

These people believe that they should only get the crumbs and not the entrée, so their behavior will be such, to ensure that they only receive crumbs. These individuals might be in a position where there are bonuses given for higher performance – "free money," as soon as one achieves a goal. However, they will not strive to achieve that goal and therefore won't receive the bonus, which allows these individuals to reinforce that nothing good ever happens to them.

However, when something goes wrong, when they are facing a crisis or are stressed out, they go all out, eating massive amounts of horrible choices. This happens because their primary incentive is to satisfy that craving and then to be defiant and go against all medical advice and eat all the carbohydrates and sugars, they can get their hands on.

Why it Works!
Maureen Pisani Ph.D.
www.ProThriveSBH.com

These people know that these choices are awful for them, but remember, they believe that they don't deserve anything good. As this is happening, these people get a momentary reprieve from the stress only to have it all return with the force of a tsunami, when their bodies respond negatively to all that ingested junk. This is when A1C levels skyrocket, when cholesterol levels go through the roof, when bad things happen to their physical bodies.

As their bodies' breakdown starts, all the new diagnoses and all the subsequent health and life repercussions only solidify these peoples' statement that nothing good ever happens to them.

THE OTHER F

-   High Levels of Self-Esteem & *The Other F*

-

This combination of traits creates individuals who know that they deserve the best in life. These people live life appreciating what's available and choosing the very best, knowing that they deserve it.

Why it Works!
Maureen Pisani Ph.D.
www.ProThriveSBH.com

71

They live by the motto "you get what you pay for," and have absolutely no problem paying a little more to receive a higher quality of product. They are also aware that choosing the best of qualities will enhance their lifestyle and quality of life, which makes it all worthwhile.

The people who have this combination will not only live a great life, but will also invest time, thought, and effort into whom they have relationships with. They know how they deserve to be treated, so if they are treated otherwise, the relationship is over, because they know they deserve better.

When stressed out or facing a crisis, the extrovert will look for sex but only with their romantic partners, because for them, it's not just sex, but a whole-body experience. These extroverts need much more than just a "hook-up," they need to make love. For these people, the coital experience takes on the body *and* mind.

Their togetherness time with their partner is a deepening of their love for each other, so it's never seen as a superficial connection, but an experience that transcends time and space.

Why it Works!
Maureen Pisani Ph.D.
www.ProThriveSBH.com

So, even in a crisis, these extroverts need that intense connection. They know what being loved at 100% feels like and anything short of that is unacceptable.

The introverts on the other hand have that internal buildup of sexual desire, and they know that they deserve the best, but in their case, having sex with their romantic partner might be too predictable and too mundane to be categorized as "the best possible" experience. These introverts equate quality of experience with how new and exciting the experience was.

Yes, in their mind they still love their romantic partners. Introvert people feel that they are honoring their commitment to their romantic partners by the lifestyle they are providing them, which to them is proportionate to how much they love them.

When stressed out, these introverts, although initially focused on the project/crisis that needs to be handled, will look for sex once the stressor is manageable.

Why it Works!
Maureen Pisani Ph.D.
www.ProThriveSBH.com

73

Yes, they might have sex with their romantic partners, but they might also look for coworkers/colleagues, because a new sexual partner offers the excitement and unpredictability they crave and enjoy. Yes, they might even resort to hiring professional sex workers to get the sexual experience they believe they deserve. To these introvert people, the release comes from the knowing that they did receive the best.

- Low Levels of Self-Esteem and *The Other F* -

This combination of traits creates individuals who have received the short end of the stick one too many times. These people are at a point in their lives where whatever they receive is acceptable to them. They function on the "that'll do" attitude.

This low expectation usually starts during childhood, where hand-me-downs, second-hand goods, and even knock-offs are seen as appropriate and satisfactory for the individuals by the adults in their lives. By the time they're adults, these people live their lives with low expectations, generally drifting through life knowing that their lives are probably going to be mediocre, or at best - average.

Why it Works!
Maureen Pisani Ph.D.
www.ProThriveSBH.com

When life is going smoothly, these people go about their day not expecting much. They do their work, knowing that it'll do, believing that what they're producing is just enough. They're usually not expecting to be highlighted as the employee of the month or given a commendation or even offered a promotion. It's never happened to them before, so why should it now? They believe that they are meant to be in the background. Basically, they see themselves as a worker-bee, as average.

When facing a crisis or feeling stressed out, these people find themselves in a quandary.

On the one hand, they are so stressed that they appreciate that something just has to happen, but on the other hand, they believe that that they don't deserve the best outcome possible.

The extrovert people will therefore look for sexual encounters, but they won't be very selective. In fact, these extroverts are unconsciously looking for sexual experiences that will be remembered as mediocre, because that's what they truly believe they deserve.

Why it Works!
Maureen Pisani Ph.D.
www.ProThriveSBH.com

75

Now, as you by now understand, mediocre sex for the extroverts will only increase their stress, so they will find themselves looking for more sexual partners. Yet, because they are functioning from their limiting beliefs, they will only find connections that always feel incomplete.

These extroverts might find the solution to their stress when they connect with someone in a "friends with benefits" situation. These extrovert people with low self-esteem might believe that they are not worthy of being in a true loving committed relationship where they are treated in the best of ways, so the friends with benefits scenario offers them a constant person, but without what their heart desires the most – commitment and love.

When stressed out or facing a crisis, introverts find themselves in a loop. There's a part of them that's wired to focus on the crisis, resolve and re-establish that sense of being in control, but there's another part of them that believes that they are not deserving of the best outcome possible.

Why it Works!
Maureen Pisani Ph.D.
www.ProThriveSBH.com

They will therefore search for sexual encounters which could also include one-nightstands, because in that setting, the introverts will have the newness of the experience which works as a magnificent aphrodisiac, but it's also with a total stranger, so if the stress level is too high and climax doesn't occur, their secret is safe.

Introvert ladies, when stressed out, have a difficult time climaxing, so to save face and not to hurt their extrovert sexual partner's feelings, they will tend to fake the orgasm, in order to conclude the interlude as fast as possible.

They might take matters into their own hands and once sexual release has been achieved, they can return to working on resolving their crisis. However, keep in mind, that because of their low levels of self-esteem, they will refrain from striving to resolve the crisis fully, and as soon as the temporary solution they came up with resulted in a level of peace that seemed acceptable to them, they will stop.

Why it Works!
Maureen Pisani Ph.D.
www.ProThriveSBH.com

77

SELF-ACCEPTANCE

FIGHT

- High Levels of Self-Acceptance and Fight -

This combination of traits creates people who take action (Fight) and also know what they can and cannot do. These individuals come across as practical people, always eager to learn because they know where the line in the sand is for them. These people are honest, forthright, and share quite easily when they take over a project or when they need to contact someone else to do that part of the process.

These people are realists. They know what strengths and weaknesses they have and are quite comfortable with them. Yes, they will always be working on improving themselves, but for the most part they like themselves on an "as-is" basis. These individuals can appreciate that they are a masterpiece *and* a work-in-progress simultaneously.

In relationships, these people are aware of their downsides and work on being as fair as possible with their romantic partner. However, these people don't appreciate or enjoy when a weakness is thrown in their face in an accusatory manner.

Why it Works!
Maureen Pisani Ph.D.
www.ProThriveSBH.com

These people already know about their weaknesses, so being insulted and put down for something they are already aware of just adds insult to injury.

In extreme cases, the extremely high levels of self-acceptance might create a persona who puts more value on the negative aspects/ the weaknesses they perceive to have, instead of seeing the strengths and weaknesses as characteristics one can be happy about or work on. Because these individuals are so aware, they might undermine their strengths because of how present the weaknesses are in their everyday life. These people are so aware of the weaknesses that they highlight them to the point where their weaknesses will outshine any possible strengths that they might have.

- Low Levels of Self-Acceptance and Fight -

This combination of traits creates individuals who live most of their life in denial. Usually this occurs when during the imprint years (0-8 years of age), adults commented on how they were behaving and gave the child labels/titles that, even though the child knew at that time that those labels/titles were incorrect, the child deferred to the adults' wisdom and accepted them.

Why it Works!
Maureen Pisani Ph.D.
www.ProThriveSBH.com

79

It's quite a common occurrence for a child to have accepted a label/title given to them during the first 8 years of their lives,

because the rationalization is that "_____" loves me, so if "_____" is saying that I'm "_____," they must be right.

Even as children we are discerning, so if a stranger or someone we interacted with rarely commented negatively about us, we usually can disregard the comment and keep going on with our lives. However, if a parent, grandparent, relative, teacher, older sibling, or even close classmate said something to us, that would carry more weight. The closer the relationship, the stronger the bond, the more we love them, and the more they love us. All these aspects combine to make an off-hand comment become a label/title written in stone that we carry for the rest of our lives.

Remember, our unconscious mind is formed during these first eight years of life. For most of us, our first memory is around age five. However, we all know that we lived each day before our first memory, meaning that we experienced, witnessed, and heard countless situations, all of which are stored in our unconscious mind. We might not realize what those experiences were, but our unconscious mind's chords still get plucked and still resonate whenever a similar situation arises.

Why it Works!
Maureen Pisani Ph.D.
www.ProThriveSBH.com

The individuals with low self-acceptance will work tremendously hard to improve but have a very difficult time accepting their strengths. They struggle with why they should invest in themselves, because regardless of what they achieve they will always still see themselves as less than.

This low self-acceptance usually starts in childhood, following an emotionally painful experience. The child usually blames himself/herself for whatever the situation was, and at that young age, makes the decision that they don't like themselves. Never does the child think that they are still a child and that they might wish to have the option to re-visit that situation once they're completely grown up. The decision was made, and that child has lived their life bouncing every thought, decision, and action off that hasty erroneous conclusion.

Please keep in mind that as an organ, the brain keeps growing until we're 24 years old. Unfortunately, most labels/titles that affect our everyday life were given to us and we accepted them way before we ever reached 24.

Why it Works!
Maureen Pisani Ph.D.
www.ProThriveSBH.com

81

FLIGHT

- High Levels of Self-Acceptance and Flight
-

This combination of traits creates people who appreciate who they truly are and use the escape mechanism Flight to walk out of situations.

They know what they can do and what is out of their capabilities. They might share that they are not good at something, and if placed in a situation where they need to do something that is out of their wheelhouse, these people will walk away, or at the very least come up with some sickness that will remove them from the situation if only on a temporary basis.

These people, being so aware of their strengths and weaknesses, don't enjoy being put in situations where they have to face or expose their weaknesses, especially in professional situations. So as soon as the stress starts building, they will come up with some excuse to remove themselves from that situation. Sometimes with high levels of stress, these people experience health crises that make it impossible to stay, so the triggering of the survival mechanism is not only the only way out, but the obvious way to help deal with the health situation.

Why it Works!
Maureen Pisani Ph.D.
www.ProThriveSBH.com

- Low Levels of Self-Acceptance and Flight -

This combination of traits creates people who understand that they had a bumpy past and blame themselves for whatever current situation they find themselves in. These individuals are aware of all the mistakes they have made, and so are incredibly self-judgmental.

They only see the bad in themselves and don't even consider the possibility that there's some good inside. They think the worst of themselves and are their worst critic, constantly.

To make matters worse, as soon as these people are confronted with something to do... being that they truly believe that they have nothing good inside, stress is triggered instantly and then these individuals do what seems to be the only way to react – escape, leave, or walk away from the situation.

This behavior creates a lose-lose situation in which they have to remove themselves from any potential opportunity. These people's history is usually loaded with negative experiences where negative, judgmental labels were given. Over time they began to believe these labels, and now they function from that negative perspective.

Why it Works!
Maureen Pisani Ph.D.
www.ProThriveSBH.com

83

FREEZE

- High Levels of Self- Acceptance & Freeze
-

This combination of traits creates people who are fully aware of their strengths and weaknesses. They are individuals who like themselves when everything is going smoothly.

They know what behavior is acceptable to them, where the line of propriety is, and what they will or won't do.

When life is good – work is going well and the relationship is going well, everything is good. These people are fully functional and can relate and respond positively to all kinds of positive scenarios.

However, if a negative situation arises, these individuals will freeze and not respond. This could occur in either a personal or professional situation. If they find themselves in a confrontational situation, they will freeze.

Internally, they know what should be said or done, but they simply cannot move a muscle. We each have Freeze as a possible survival mechanism, but when these people here have Freeze as their primary response, it's usually because early in childhood when they were facing a traumatic situation,

Why it Works!
Maureen Pisani Ph.D.
www.ProThriveSBH.com

Freezing turned out to be the best response for them. Being that these people internalize every stressful situation as a life-or-death scenario, knowing that Freeze saved their life once, makes Freeze the preferred unconscious choice.

Unfortunately, nowadays the 'life-or-death' scenarios are few and far between, but internally these individuals respond to any stressful situation, crisis, or confrontation with the same intensity and therefore with the same 'tried and true' technique.

This doesn't work well for these people, because their colleagues or romantic partners don't understand how they can just stand there and do/say nothing. This misunderstood passivity hurts these individuals more than anything that they could have possibly said or done.

- Low Levels of Self- Acceptance and Freeze -

This combination of traits creates people who cannot or truly don't know how to accept themselves. Even if they are having a phenomenal day, internally there's a sense of guilt that they are being treated in a way that is too good for them. If everything is going smoothly, these individuals believe that at some point someone will realize how bad of a person they truly are, and everything in their life will crumble.

Why it Works!
Maureen Pisani Ph.D.
www.ProThriveSBH.com

85

This lack of self-acceptance usually begins in early childhood. Children usually compare themselves to their siblings, classmates, and friends. They are observant primarily to confirm that they are treated in a similar fashion to their siblings, because then they have confirmation that they belong. However, each of us is unique, so comparisons can only go so far. The situation worsens when the child becomes aware of how one or both parents (and/or grandparents) treat the other siblings better and not themselves.

If one of the parents dotes on one child, but ignores or minimizes the other's accomplishments, the neglected child will notice the discrepancy and feel the sting of rejection but can't come to an educated decision. Even though he/she is still only a child, the only natural conclusion the child can come to is "I did something wrong," or "It's my fault," or "I'm a bad kid." As soon as the child comes to those erroneous conclusions, he/she will think negatively of himself/herself for the rest of his/her life (unless he/she seeks therapy to rectify it later in life). This lack of acceptance is running in these people's unconscious minds as their foundation 24/7, even on their good days.

Why it Works!
Maureen Pisani Ph.D.
www.ProThriveSBH.com

When a crisis occurs or work life is stressful, these people will instantly blame themselves, and from prior experience will freeze. When these individuals freeze, they become quiet, and they believe that they will fade into the background and everything will return to a safe, peaceful, calm normal.

What these individuals don't realize is that when they freeze, this lack of participation, this silence, this lack of response only infuriates the other party and things get worse. The other person in the situation is expecting these people to respond and when they don't, it is usually construed to mean that they don't care.

Internally, these people would like nothing more than to speak up, voice their opinion, and/or take a stand, but because of Freeze being triggered, they are incapable of any of those choices. This inability to respond only strengthens their lack of self-acceptance, which keeps these people stuck in their self-destructive loop.

Why it Works!
Maureen Pisani Ph.D.
www.ProThriveSBH.com

87

FOOD

- High Levels of Self-Acceptance and Food -

This combination of traits creates individuals who are quite aware of the person they are and are comfortable acknowledging their strengths easily. When life is going smoothly, these people will be aware that they are slightly overweight, but are quite accepting of it, joking about the fact that there's more than enough of them to go around. They might be aware of enjoying food a little too much but would rather label themselves as 'foodies' than anything else. These individuals will also be aware of the benefits healthy foods offer, and where and when it's acceptable in their mind to choose more decadent choices and why. These people will splurge on a celebratory dinner, where the choice is determined by how much celebrating they are planning on, rather than how they will be feeling later that night, during the night or even the next morning.

When these people are stressed out and/or are facing a crisis, they will instinctively choose which foods to self-soothe with. These individuals will have lists, albeit mental, of what to eat according to which crisis they are facing. The choices of foods they ingest will usually be proportional to which stressor they are facing, or according to how intense the stressor is, and/or how easily attainable the solution is.

Why it Works!
Maureen Pisani Ph.D.
www.ProThriveSBH.com

- Low Levels of Self-Acceptance and Food -

This combination of traits creates people who already don't accept who they are, other than the negative aspects of themselves. They have been told so many times how deficient, substandard, and incompetent they are, that these individuals now believe that they are truly just a massive disappointment to themselves and everyone else.

When life is going smoothly, they will still not make wise decisions on food choices, because they don't care what the resultant outcome is. They don't choose foods for their health value, but according to what will make them temporarily feel better.

They will internally rationalize that because they are such a disappointment to themselves and to others, it really doesn't matter what they eat, how healthy they are, or how long they get to live, because nobody cares anyway… including themselves.

When these individuals are stressed out or facing a crisis, then all pseudo-control goes out the window.

Why it Works!
Maureen Pisani Ph.D.
www.ProThriveSBH.com

89

They will gorge on whatever is within reach to simply diminish the pain the stress is causing. When these people have such low self-acceptance levels, they see themselves in such a bad light that eating the worst choice doesn't even raise a red flag. (Imagine a diabetic eating a dozen doughnuts in one sitting without blinking an eye.)

When they overeat, they are fully aware that they are overdoing it, but because they already don't like themselves, it truly doesn't matter to them, if they gain more weight, get sicker, or risk their life. All these people are focused on is eating what they want without restrictions, knowing that at least initially, there will be relief.

THE OTHER F

- High Levels of Self-Acceptance and *The Other F* -

This combination of traits creates individuals who know who they are in all aspects of life. They know that they are evolving humans, and therefore accept that they have both strengths and weaknesses, and that they have good and bad habits.

Why it Works!
Maureen Pisani Ph.D.
www.ProThriveSBH.com

They are very aware and proud of what they consider to be their strengths, and because of their high levels of self-acceptance, they will expose their weaknesses as a badge of honor to display how human they are. They are aware that they are conquering several learning curves simultaneously, and so they love and appreciate themselves by giving themselves permission to falter, fall, and sometimes even go splat (face flat into the mud), as long as they get up and go for it again.

When life is going smoothly, these individuals live a good life. They're happy, easygoing, and they enjoy every aspect of life. To the extrovert people, sex is a regular/daily experience where they are loved and accepted for who they truly are. These extroverts are open to enhancing their sexual repertoire because the better at sex they are, the more they'll impress their partner, and therefore the more their partner will love them, which is the ultimate success for them.

To the introvert people, sex is also on a regular basis, but it's usually a scheduled event, even if it's only scheduled in the introvert's mind. These introverts whose primary focus is career with high levels of self-acceptance are aware that a good life includes everything, including a happy and satisfied partner.

Why it Works!
Maureen Pisani Ph.D.
www.ProThriveSBH.com

91

Having a happy and satisfied romantic partner will result in the introvert people having a calmer personal life. When the introvert's partner (who is usually an extrovert) starts feeling neglected or sexually deprived, the partner will make their displeasure known to the introvert people, which will disrupt their schedule and distract them from their main focus – succeeding even more in their career. So the introvert people will have sex with their extrovert partners to keep the home environment peaceful and calm.

- Low Levels of Self-Acceptance and
The Other F -

This combination of traits creates individuals who not only don't accept who they are but dislike themselves. They probably only accept the negative aspects of their personalities, so when *The Other F* survival mechanism is triggered, these people won't choose their partners wisely. Their behavior is reflective of how much they don't accept themselves.

When life is going smoothly, these extroverts who thrive on acceptance and will go to any lengths to prevent rejection but behave in a way that creates self-rejection.

Why it Works!
Maureen Pisani Ph.D.
www.ProThriveSBH.com

This is incredibly painful for these people. The only solution they see is to hook up with someone because that sexual connection will soothe and temporarily make life better.

Unfortunately, because these extrovert people think of love and sex as interchangeable, this impersonal sexual connection will initially soothe their need. But from a long-term perspective, this behavior will only leave them feeling even more rejected, and in an aspect of their life that they value immensely.

These individuals are caught in a contradiction of scenarios. On one hand, they don't accept that they are deserving of a good, solid, positive, supportive, loving relationship, so they usually aren't in a committed relationship; but on the other hand, that's exactly what they desire the most. Even though they secretly dream of being in a committed, supportive, loving relationship, they will choose casual, non-committed, sporadic, hookups due to their 'fix-it-now' attitude, which will invariably leave them in the space they believe they deserve to be...not getting what they want.

When these extrovert people are stressed out or are facing a crisis and *The Other F* survival mechanism is triggered, then there's a compounding effect, because both triggers are going for the same solution.

Why it Works!
Maureen Pisani Ph.D.
www.ProThriveSBH.com

93

These people know that they need sex, and they need it now. However, because of their low levels of self-acceptance, they choose unwisely, where location and availability of a potential partner overrides whether this partner is suitable for them or not. In fact, if the potential sexual partner is not suitable for them, then choosing that person falls in alignment with their low self-acceptance. As you might surmise, this will only lead to these people being repeatedly heart-broken. After the sex is over, and the sexual partner (usually an introvert) walks away, these individuals are shocked by how heartless the other person was. This happens because the extroverts cannot comprehend how the introvert separates sex and love. So, even though the extrovert people promised that the hookup was a "no-strings-attached" situation, in actuality, they still admit to having feelings for the sexual partner.

When introvert people are facing a crisis or are stressed out and *The Other F* is triggered, they are again pulled in two opposite directions. On one hand, they would rather focus on work and get the job done, but their low levels of self-acceptance undermine their momentum, because to live the life they think they deserve, they cannot succeed to the max.

Why it Works!
Maureen Pisani Ph.D.
www.ProThriveSBH.com

On the other hand, these people are aware of the sexual tension that's building up. If the introvert is in a relationship, then they might initiate sex, which is unusual; but if these people are single, then they have two options. Either they find a willing participant, usually an extrovert who is always ready, willing, and able to enjoy a sexual experience any day and any time, or if time constraints are intensifying the pressure, masturbation is chosen as the best recourse, because it's efficient and effective.

Why it Works!
Maureen Pisani Ph.D.
www.ProThriveSBH.com

95

SELF-WORTH

FIGHT

- High levels of Self-Worth and Fight -

This combination of traits results in people who are go-getters and individuals who know what they bring to the table and know that they are worthy of the best. These individuals have invested in themselves, and therefore know that with every step up, their worth has increased. These people will have no problem raising their fees because they know that the more training, experience, and wisdom they have, the more value they have to offer.

These individuals understand that for them to rise and differentiate themselves from others, higher levels of training are required, and upon completion, a higher sense of self-worth is established internally. These people are extremely factual about their accomplishments and are usually quite down to earth, until pushed or in a crisis. Then they will go for what they believe their worth is.

When facing a crisis or stress, these people will take action. They will assess the situation, strategize, plan for all possible outcomes, and then implement the plan.

Why it Works!
Maureen Pisani Ph.D.
www.ProThriveSBH.com

They understand that the crisis is basically an opportunity to learn from, so they approach it with the best ending in mind.

- Low Levels of Self-Worth and Fight -

This combination of traits creates people who are triggered to take action, but at the same time they don't believe that they deserve the desired outcome. These individuals will work hard, but then fall short on something incredibly minor. They will wish for success, will even work for success, but then at the 11th hour will have something happen to stop them from making it to the very top of the success ladder.

These individuals might succeed to an extent where they are aware of not being the #1 person. In fact, knowing that there's someone else who is more successful than they are might actually give these people the loophole to succeed to a level that is in alignment with their low level of self-worth. These people will even rationalize that that level of success is more than enough for them.

When facing a crisis, these individuals' survival mechanism's response is to take action, but their low levels of self-worth will put the brakes on anything they might have come up with as a solution.

Why it Works!
Maureen Pisani Ph.D.
www.ProThriveSBH.com

97

In their own minds, these people believe that they aren't worthy of success, so they will act out in other ways – shouting, swearing, punching holes into the walls, basically making a big show of supposedly taking action, but not in a way that will handle or resolve the crisis.

FLIGHT

- High Levels of Self-Worth and Flight -

This combination of traits creates people who are inclined to hide, walk away, and escape rather than fight for what they deserve, even though they truly believe they are worthy. This combination creates a tremendous amount of frustration because the traits are quite opposing.

On one hand, these people instinctively feel the need to walk away, get away from the stressful scenarios, while on the other hand, these individuals' high levels of self-worth push them to go for it, do the work, strive for it, the result being that one of the drives will win, resulting in them always feeling like something's missing.

When stressed out, and their survival mechanisms are triggered, they will over-ride everything and anything else that these people believe.

Why it Works!
Maureen Pisani Ph.D.
www.ProThriveSBH.com

They will have things happen, where they will be incapable of handling or resolving the crisis. Whether they leave the location, pass out, or come down with a panic attack/migraine, something will happen where these people will not be functional.

Please keep in mind that it's all unconscious. These people are not intentionally planning any of their responses. To them, these behaviors, just happen.

- Low Levels of Self-Worth and Flight -

This combination of traits creates people who are wired to escape everything and anything that creates any stress or has the possibility of improving their life. These individuals function from the perspective that they are not worth much, so little effort is made to improve. These people are seen as unmotivated, and function only within what has been their history.

These people know that there are others who have a much better life than they do, but deep down inside they truly believe that where they work, and how they live, is good enough. They live with the "that will do" attitude. These people will never strive for more than what they have been accustomed to. These people work off of what their family raised them in, so if as children,

Why it Works!
Maureen Pisani Ph.D.
www.ProThriveSBH.com

99

they were raised in a "just enough" household, where they had the basic amenities, but everything was secondhand, rickety but made do, that's the standard of living these people believe they should be living in nowadays.

These peoples' low levels of self-worth also show up in how they never ask for a raise or strive for a promotion. In fact, if given a promotion, they will either decline it, begrudgingly accept it, or do the job so bad, that they are soon demoted to the old position.

These individuals' normal method of functioning is to do the bare minimum to not get fired. They know that they need a job to survive, but they will never strive to rise up from the level in which they were raised.

FREEZE

- High Levels of Self-Worth and Freeze -

This combination of traits creates individuals who know what their worth is but expect everyone else to behave in a way that is in alignment with their belief. When things are going smoothly, these people function exceptionally well. They will climb the corporate ladder quickly, knowing that they deserve the best and that they are worthy of the best.

Why it Works!
Maureen Pisani Ph.D.
www.ProThriveSBH.com

However, if a crisis occurs, or deadlines are coming up, these people will freeze. Instead of working harder, when under stress, they will have migraines, will come down with some illness that will require them to stay at home. In a difficult situation these individuals won't be able to function and in fact will completely stop functioning.

(Please keep in mind, that all this is triggered from their unconscious mind. They never plan any of this. What they experience is incredibly painful and real.)

In a relationship, these people know how they should be treated, but if the other partner pulls a stunt, insults, or hurts them, they will just freeze and won't respond. Once the crisis or the argument calms down, these people will be riddled with the "I should have said/ I should have done" self-inflicted guilt-trip. They will think about what they could have or should have done, but in reality, they are fully aware that they will never step up or speak up for themselves.

These people truly don't understand why they don't or cannot respond, because internally they know that they are truly worthy. These opposing characteristics result in repeated self-disappointing behavior.

Why it Works!
Maureen Pisani Ph.D.
www.ProThriveSBH.com

101

- Low Levels of Self-Worth and Freeze -

This combination of traits creates people who truly don't believe they are worth much. To add insult to injury, when a crisis occurs and/or they feel stressed, they will simply not respond, not react, and not speak up, but stay silent, passive, and nonreactive.

Usually, in these peoples' childhood, something had to have happened that imprinted on them that they weren't worthy of something. It could have been that a request for an expensive gift was declined, or a repeated negative cutting comment was given for whatever they asked for. Sometimes, the dysfunction of the family imprints onto the child's unconscious mind. So, if one child gets great presents while the other child gets average "stuff" (nothing that the child had desired or was appropriate), the child might surmise that he/she isn't as worthy as the other sibling.

It could also be that these individuals' parents overcompensated for something and coddled the child, giving them everything. Initially, the child enjoys the pampering treatment, but eventually this pattern backfires terribly, because as the child grows and sees their classmates' accomplishing things, they become very aware that they haven't accomplished the same skills.

Why it Works!
Maureen Pisani Ph.D.
www.ProThriveSBH.com

The child goes past the fact that their parents were catering to them hand and foot but comes to the sad realization that apparently their parents didn't believe that they could accomplish those skills. This scenario creates humans who don't have the capability to accomplish the normal chores of life.

These individuals are fully aware that they cannot do normal life stuff – balance a check book, cook their own meals, plan their financial future, manage their own home, be financially responsible, or be in charge of their life, so the conclusion they come to repeatedly is that they are not worthy. Instead of looking at this scenario as a learning opportunity, because of their freeze survival mechanism, they will simply stagnate in this situation. If these people are single, then this situation will spiral out of control soon as the last parent dies.

If these individuals are in a relationship, the partner will either be incredibly frustrated and will be forced into running everything – the household, the finances, the relationship - and look at them as dead weight and just accept it for what it is. However, most of the time as soon as the partner realizes that this is a pattern, that this was not because their partner had a bad day at work or was in a bad mood, but that their partner's inertia is a permanent behavior, the individual leaves.

Why it Works!
Maureen Pisani Ph.D.
www.ProThriveSBH.com

103

These people usually have a menial job, one that they have been doing for decades. It is a job that was acceptable and approved by the parents, and so these individuals felt comfortable doing that job. Over the years, even the repetition of the job helped these people get accustomed to it and so they usually do have a job, but it will never be one of constant growth or advancement, but rather one of repetition and stagnation. These individuals are usually so stuck in a rut and are so comfortable in this proverbial rut that they will furnish it.

FOOD

- High Levels of Self-Worth and Food -

This combination of traits creates people who are aware that they are worthy of a good life, a good body, and good health. While life is going smoothly, these individuals will be cognizant of their food choices, always taking extra precaution to choose which food combinations will offer them the best subsequent results.

These people are aware of the principle called "The Slight Edge," in which the slightest of daily positive

Why it Works!
Maureen Pisani Ph.D.
www.ProThriveSBH.com

efforts will result in a huge upswing in the future; while the mildest of bad habits practiced daily (or at least regularly) will cause devastating results at some point in the future.

When these people face a crisis or are stressed out and their survival mechanism FOOD is triggered, they will definitely resort to food to self-soothe. However, even though they are eating more than usual and for the wrong reasons (food never solves any major problems), these people will still be aware of the choices of food they are ingesting.

These people might choose to have sugar-free candy This way they ARE eating candy, but it's not loaded with tons of sugar; or they might choose the biggest pizza with all the toppings, but it will have a cauliflower crust, which tempers the potential negative hit.

These individuals are aware that they are stressed out and know that self-soothing always feels good, but they are also aware that the stress will at some point diminish and at that point they still are worthy of living a good life, with good health and a good body. So, even in the worst of times, these people will never just lose control and eat whatever, whenever, in whatever quantities feel good at the time. No, they will self-soothe with bigger portions than normal, but with wise choices of food.

Why it Works!
Maureen Pisani Ph.D.
www.ProThriveSBH.com

105

This combination of traits creates people who don't believe that they are worthy of anything good. When life is going smoothly, these individuals will already indulge and make unwise food choices. These people are coming from a painful place where they cannot see their own worth, so investing in oneself by choosing healthy foods to eat isn't high on their priority list.

This negative self-identity label usually is given in early childhood. If the negative comments continue through later years, the adult has a library of memories reinforcing that they are truly unworthy.

When these people are stressed out or are facing a crisis, then they lose complete control. This is when these individuals will binge on massive amounts of the worst food combinations possible, fully aware that they are the wrong choices and that eating will definitely make things worse, but they couldn't care less about their future outcomes, and so continue to overeat. All this is usually done in a desperate attempt to self-soothe, so the higher the stress, the more painful the emotions, the more they eat of the worst choices of food possible.

The self-soothing relief is unfortunately temporary, ranging from a few minutes to a couple of hours at best.

Why it Works!
Maureen Pisani Ph.D.
www.ProThriveSBH.com

Once the pancreas starts releasing insulin to metabolize all the excess sugar, the desired pseudo-calmness retreats, and they land with a hard thud back into reality, facing the stressor. Only this time around, they will have solidified the low levels of self-worth because of the prior binging episode, so all they would have accomplished is the reinforcing of the negative label of their self-identity.

THE OTHER F

- High Levels of Self-Worth & *The Other F* -

This combination of traits creates people who live life through the lens of knowing how much they believe they are worth. These individuals have invested in themselves and have an outstanding track record of what they've accomplished. They usually have a stellar reputation, so it's more than understandable when they live their personal and professional lives according to set standards.

They have healthy boundaries, so the people with whom they interact are positive, responsible people who celebrate them, who appreciate them, and whose collaboration is synergistic thereby offering win-win situations for everyone involved.

Why it Works!
Maureen Pisani Ph.D.
www.ProThriveSBH.com

107

These individuals know where the line in the sand is and refuse to cross it, because the repercussions will not only be unsavory, but will create situations that will be demeaning and hurtful for them.

When life is going smoothly, these people are productive, positive, efficient, dependable, respectful, and beyond professional, because they understand that what they give they will receive. They know that they are worthy of receiving the best, so they give the best.

However, when the extrovert people are facing a crisis and are stressed out, and they feel that sexual urge intensify, they know that to relax they need that exquisite sexual release, but if they're single, finding the person who is in alignment with how worthy they feel they are can sometimes be difficult. When the stress level intensifies and reaches its breaking point, extroverts will override their usual pickiness in choosing partners and will find someone who they hope is up to their caliber. As much as the extrovert people are into commitment and long-term relationships, when the stress reaches boiling point levels, as long as their partner is attractive, hot, sexy, and is into them, then it's "game on."

Why it Works!
Maureen Pisani Ph.D.
www.ProThriveSBH.com

When the introvert people are facing a crisis or are stressed out, they end up feeling like there's a part of them that needs to tackle the buildup of sexual need, while another part of them feels like they have to focus on work and career. The introverts know that they are worthy of having continuous improvement in their career, followed by continuous upgrades in their lives. So, most will ignore the intensifying sexual urge in preference of working on resolving the crisis. However, if resolution is prolonged, then the sexual need will have to be addressed. The introvert people will either (according to time constraints) give in to having sex with their romantic partners, in an attempt to achieve release, and if nothing else, give themselves temporary relaxation. However, if there are time constraints and the introvert people are stuck in the office, on location, or on a 48/36/72-hour shift, then connecting with a colleague (as improper as that might seem to most) will be seen as an efficient solution to the introvert individuals.

Keep in mind that the introvert people are able split love and sex, so in their mind, they still love their romantic partner, but their physical body needed sexual release, so the colleague ended up being the right person, at the right time, at the right place.

Why it Works!
Maureen Pisani Ph.D.
www.ProThriveSBH.com

109

The introvert individuals really can compartmentalize it to that extent. When they say, "it meant nothing," they truly mean it because they see it just as an action to prevent brain fog and/or headaches.

- Low Levels of Self-Worth and *The Other F*

This combination of traits creates people who, although they have worked tremendously hard in their lives, the results produced have been so disappointing, that they believe that that's all their worth.

Whether it's a cultural inheritance or a discriminatory slur, these people have gone through such negative experiences, where they have either been told that they're unworthy, or the actions of others have convinced them that they're unworthy, regardless of whether it was opinions or facts that these people have faced, they currently believe that they're unworthy. This is a true shame, because I believe that everyone IS worthy of the best.

When life is going smoothly, these individuals are living life not expecting much. They drift through day after day, secretly hoping that something might improve, but

Why it Works!
Maureen Pisani Ph.D.
www.ProThriveSBH.com

realizing with every disappointment that what they were told had to be true, because the mediocre results they received today, yet again, prove that they're unworthy.

When these people are stressed out or facing a crisis, and they connect with that sexual need, they know what it's going to take to feel calm again. However, because of their low levels of self-worth, choosing a sexual partner might not be as stringent of a process, as most would like to believe.

The extrovert people who know that sexual release is the best cure for everything will find the first available partner who is interested and who says yes. These individuals believe that they're unworthy of finding the best possible choice, so to stay in their unconscious comfort zone, they will hook up with whomever they encounter. These hookups are simply sexual connections, with no strings attached. As much as the extrovert individuals proclaim to be "modern" and "detached" from all that emotional attachment scenario, they can't help themselves. As soon as the extrovert people have sex, they feel an emotional attachment and they believe that they've fallen in love with that person, and so are devastated when that person (usually an introvert individual) walks away without blinking an eye.

Why it Works!
Maureen Pisani Ph.D.
www.ProThriveSBH.com

111

These extroverts who chose rapidly and unwisely because of the intense stress level find themselves time and time again in dilemmas where they went into the hookup scenario for the quick sex solution, and then left with their heart broken yet again. However, when they're going through the grieving process over the hookup, which in their mind has now been transformed into "the relationship that was never given a chance to blossom," they rationalize it internally as the outcome they believe they deserve.

The introvert people who, because of their stress level, would rather work on their crisis to resolve it will initially push away the thought of sex. But as the stress intensifies, caution is thrown to the wind and the introvert individuals will seek and find someone to have sex with. And that's exactly what it will be – just sex.

These introverts have a mental list of what to do to please their partner sexually, but that "mental sex list" is only implemented if and when the introverts either want to impress their partner or they are ready to commit to their extrovert sexual partner, because being in a committed relationship will eventually help them move up in their career.

However, when the high levels of stress are running the show, the introvert individuals will find a partner and be extremely selfish in how they have sex.

Why it Works!
Maureen Pisani Ph.D.
www.ProThriveSBH.com

They are connecting with this other person for one purpose and one purpose only - to achieve a sexual climax that will hopefully release and reduce the levels of stress within. So, the other person's needs are nowhere in their awareness. These introvert people will go into the sexual interlude with only their release in mind, so even if the other person might be ready for a love-making session, all they will receive is a brief intense series of movements where the introvert people achieve climax quickly and are gone before the partners' blood pressure resets to calm.

Because of the low levels of self-worth, the introvert people won't choose wisely, so the sexual partner (who feels used by the end of this scenario) will make their displeasure known publicly. This will only retrigger higher levels of stress, but the introvert people will rationalize all this internally as them receiving what they deserve.

Why it Works!
Maureen Pisani Ph.D.
www.ProThriveSBH.com

113

SELF-RESPECT

FIGHT

- High Levels of Self-Respect and Fight -

This combination of traits creates people who are not only go-getters but are also aware of what's appropriate and what isn't. They have a code of conduct that they live by, and this code determines how they behave in every aspect of life. There are certain things that these people will participate in, and other things that they never will. They appreciate that lowering oneself is truly not a good thing to do. They live life to the fullest, albeit within the margins of morality and ethics. They understand that honoring themselves is so important that it's one of their top priorities. They will behave in a way that might be surprising to most, because when confronted, they will usually choose the high road and refuse to retaliate.

These people understand that they are responsible for their thoughts, decisions, and actions; and that each of them has the potential to either enhance or diminish their reputation. The high levels of self-respect tend to predetermine good, respectful behavior towards oneself and others. These individuals usually don't have a reactive response to life, but rather a proactive response that only occurs once they have evaluated the situation,

Why it Works!
Maureen Pisani Ph.D.
www.ProThriveSBH.com

gauged the pros and cons, and taken the time to understand the other person's perspective. Only then will these people respond calmly, sharing kind words. Regardless of whether the other person agrees or not, they will still choose kind words to express themselves.

They understand that there is no need to be rude, spiteful, or hurtful. These people wisely choose to speak their truth with kindness, because ultimately how they respond is on their conscience.

When these individuals are in a crisis or stressed out, they will still take action, but it will be within what they deem appropriate and respectful to themselves and to the others involved. They have the fortitude to be direct while remaining polite. They will get the message across, they will handle and resolve the situation, but it will always be with manners and etiquette.

- Low Levels of Self-Respect and Fight -

This combination of traits creates individuals who are wired to take action but really don't care about the cost. They will cut corners, cheat, lie, and deceive others to get the outcome they think they deserve. Unfortunately, these people's low levels of self-respect are exhibited by the behavior in which they engage.

Why it Works!
Maureen Pisani Ph.D.
www.ProThriveSBH.com

115

These people claim that they are in it for the thrill, but in reality, they couldn't care less how people think of or perceive them, because they don't think highly of themselves.

These individuals usually have a trigger temper, will fly off the handle for almost no reason at all, will scream, yell, cuss, swear, insult, and even go as far as involved in a physical altercation because afterwards, they can always state, "Oh I lost my cool. I lost control. Sorry."

This combination can become a volatile blend as the low self-respect translates to "no brakes" when the Fight survival mechanism is triggered. These people don't care if the situation is happening in an inappropriate location or in front of the wrong people. These individuals' low self-respect results in them thinking so low of themselves that they have no qualms about showing up and doing the wrong thing with the wrong people at the wrong time and wrong place.

When facing a crisis or feeling stressed out, these peoples' worst traits are revved up and they become unpredictable and uncontrollable. When their survival mechanism Fight kicks in, the thug in them emerges.

Why it Works!
Maureen Pisani Ph.D.
www.ProThriveSBH.com

Due to their low levels of self-respect, these individuals don't even care about the potential consequences they might face, after the crisis is over. Being fired from a job, losing a relationship, being thrown in jail, or doing time will all just confirm how they feel about themselves.

FLIGHT

- High Levels of Self-Respect and Flight -

This combination of traits creates people who appreciate that everyone should respect themselves and be respected by others. These individuals' behavior will be proper, appropriate, conservative, and of course, respectful. They will treat themselves with respect too, so they will never put themselves in situations or scenarios where they might be disrespected or insulted. These people will have standards that they live by, but if a situation occurs where things aren't quite as proper as they feel are adequate, instead of speaking up, these people will simply either resign, or come down with sickness, thereby creating a solution where they cannot participate. This way they get to honor their standards but not confront the powers that be.

Even though these people respect themselves, they are wired to find the easiest way out of an uncomfortable situation.

Why it Works!
Maureen Pisani Ph.D.
www.ProThriveSBH.com

117

When facing a crisis or feeling stressed out, their survival mechanism "Flight" will override any possible solution-finding strategy and get them to exit the scene immediately. When stressed, these people will come up with situations that force them to leave the location where the stressors are. Whether they have a chronic health condition or an acute response (like vomiting/diarrhea), something will happen where they remove themselves from ground zero.

- Low Levels of Self-Respect and Flight -

This combination of traits creates individuals who don't think highly of themselves at all. These people remember vividly all the "downs" they have lived through and judge themselves on those experiences. These people believe that they deserved those downfalls, and because those downfalls happened, they believe the worst of themselves. These individuals usually have a high level of self-hate, which leads to incredibly low levels of self-respect.

Being that these people think the worst of themselves, they usually have a low-level job or a job that they don't enjoy at all. These individuals only work for survival. They believe that they don't deserve to be treated with respect.

Why it Works!
Maureen Pisani Ph.D.
www.ProThriveSBH.com

In fact, their behavior will be self-destructive and somehow, they will always be the unluckiest person they know, where things/opportunities/deals fall through or unpredictably crash and become disasters.

As soon as things start going south, these people will not fight but succumb to the disaster. They will believe that that's the outcome they truly deserve. These people don't have the incentive to do something about the situation. They will throw in the towel and walk away from yet another failure.

When stressed out or facing a crisis, they not only find themselves in situations where they are wired to escape the stressor, but because of their low levels of self-respect, they don't even have the energy or initiative to attempt to resolve it. This usually leads to these individuals being seen as undependable where in the moment, instead of stepping up…they disappear.

FREEZE

- High Levels of Self-Respect and Freeze -

This combination of traits creates individuals who have learned what respect means from an early age. They understand the value of respecting themselves and others, so these peoples' behavior will fall within normal propriety standards.

Why it Works!
Maureen Pisani Ph.D.
www.ProThriveSBH.com

119

They will have solid boundaries and innately know how to handle themselves if those boundaries are breached. These boundaries of how these people are treated and how they treat others are ingrained within them. On the good days, when things are going smoothly, these people function professionally and with kindness and respect towards everyone else.

However, if a crisis occurs or these people are put in a stressful situation, even though they know internally what needs to be done and how the situation should be handled, they will freeze. These people will either become indisposed, do nothing (even though the situation demands a resolution), or at best do or say something that is so innocuous that everyone around them will be incredibly disappointed in them.

After the crisis is handled by someone else, these people might mention that *this* or *that* could have been done, but not during the actual crisis when it was their responsibility to deal with it. As much as these individuals value respect, they are aware that their inability to function during the crisis has cost them respect from others.

Why it Works!
Maureen Pisani Ph.D.
www.ProThriveSBH.com

- Low Levels of Self-Respect and Freeze -

This combination of traits creates individuals who have been through the wringer of life, to the point where they truly don't respect themselves at all. This is a particularly sad scenario because these people have gone through horrible situations where the people around them knew what was right and wrong and repeatedly chose to wrong them. So much so, that these individuals now believe that they don't deserve to be respected.

Please keep in mind that in the beginning of our lives, when we're children and our brains haven't fully developed yet, that's when we go through mostly new experiences, and that's when we come to conclusions about others, about situations, and mostly about ourselves.

If these people were in scenarios where there were negative people around them, or they faced situations because the family was in dire straits, or the family was facing horrendous situations and they were last on the list, or they were abused, or they overheard or witnessed bad behavior, these individuals might easily have come to the conclusion that the treatment that they received was because they were deserving of such abominable treatment.

Why it Works!
Maureen Pisani Ph.D.
www.ProThriveSBH.com

121

Our minds function through the "compared to what" mechanism, where we can determine how sweet or sour something is once we compare it to something else. However, as children when these individuals experienced abuse or negative behavior, because they didn't have a neutral or positive experience to compare it to, it's accepted as the baseline and becomes what these people believe is acceptable behavior.

Functioning with this low level of self-respect creates an expectation and a pattern of behavior for a continuous stream of disasters. Even if these individuals temporarily do things to improve their life, at the same time they will be accepting deplorable behavior from their partner, or their work conditions will be awful, but these people won't speak up because they believe that due to the fact of how bad they believe themselves to be, this behavior is what they deserve.

There are times where these people will realize that their partner's behavior is unfair or unjust, but because bringing up the topic will create even more stress in their life, these people will freeze and go on suffering in silence.

When facing a crisis, these people's survival mechanism "Freeze" is triggered, and they find themselves unable to function or respond.

Why it Works!
Maureen Pisani Ph.D.
www.ProThriveSBH.com

Even though a part of them is aware that the crisis requires a solution, or that they have to do something to resolve it, they just cannot.

In the professional world, this repeated freezing will be received as an incredibly negative response which could lead to painful repercussions, like being put on warning or even being fired. However, in the personal environment, this freezing will initially be disappointing to the romantic partner. When the partner realizes that this is this individual's usual response, either the behavior is accepted and the partner takes over and is in control of everything, or the partner will leave that person. However, because of their low levels of self-respect, these people, albeit heart-broken, still won't respond and just take the consequences silently.

FOOD

- High Levels of Self-Respect and Food -

This combination of traits creates individuals who are quite aware and appreciative of how essential respect is to a good life. These people honor others and themselves with respect. They will be a functional person in society, one who is highly respected and well thought of in the community.

Why it Works!
Maureen Pisani Ph.D.
www.ProThriveSBH.com

123

These people's choices are based on high levels of self-respect, so they will decide how to behave within boundaries of what's proper and honorable. When life is going smoothly, these people will choose foods that are beneficial for their health and/or physical build. They will also be mild in their indulging behaviors and choices while celebrating.

However, if these people are stressed out and/or are facing a crisis, they will still strive to be always in control, knowing that every action has an equal and opposite reaction. So, if they indulge and eat foods that are too rich or too high in fat, knowing that they will suffer from an upset stomach all the night, these people will refrain from those choices because they simply have way too much self-respect.

They might still overeat, but it will be with milder *offenders*. They might eat past their usual hours and might eat/drink things they haven't had in a long time, but it will still be with attention to moderation. After all, these people are looking to relieve the stress, not create additional health situations that will stress them out even more.

Why it Works!
Maureen Pisani Ph.D.
www.ProThriveSBH.com

- Low Levels of Self-Respect and Food -

This combination of traits creates people who know what behaviors and choices of food are beneficial for them but couldn't care less. Over the years, people have treated them so badly that they have lost all self-respect. These people think of themselves in the worst of ways, and so their behavior is reflective of this thinking pattern.

These people know what they need to do to be better, healthier, and live a more successful life, but unfortunately, they don't believe they deserve any better. So, when life is happy and calm, these people still don't eat healthily. They will rationalize that their body has received "___" number of calories, so that should be sufficient for the day, but those calories could be liquor, ice cream or candy!

To make matters worse, if these individuals are diabetic, the best way to minimize how bad these choices are is to refuse to check one's blood sugar levels – sheer denial. This way, the damage to the physical body is in the background and never brought front and center. Checking the levels would expose their double digit A1C levels and horrifying blood sugar levels, which would then be too blatant to ignore, so these individuals just don't do it.

Why it Works!
Maureen Pisani Ph.D.
www.ProThriveSBH.com

125

They function from the saying "ignorance is bliss." Unfortunately for these people, "ignorance" will result in horrible repercussions which could include blindness and amputation.

However, when these individuals are stressed out and/or are facing a crisis, they know exactly which food choices are the worst choices and which will have the biggest detrimental impact on their physiology, and they will choose those foods on purpose.

The low levels of self-respect innately force the worst possible choices to be made, because that's the only way these people's unconscious minds will be satisfied that things are the way they should be. These individuals truly believe they deserve the worst, so their behavior has to be in alignment with this belief. These people are aware of the consequences and potential health disasters that could be created by their uncontrollable eating of the wrong choices of food, but they couldn't care less.

Once the over-indulging is over, these people are left with a fleeting sensation of comfort and the pseudo-satisfaction of having indulged just as they had planned to. However, the lasting result of this behavior is that after each overeating session, these people just dislike themselves even more and lose a little bit more of self-respect.

Why it Works!
Maureen Pisani Ph.D.
www.ProThriveSBH.com

THE OTHER F

- High Levels of Self-Respect & *The Other F*
-

This combination of traits creates individuals who appreciate how necessary respect is, for both themselves and others. When life is going smoothly, these people function from a point of view that self-respect dictates their thoughts, decisions, and actions. These people choose wisely in every aspect of their life. They appreciate how respectful behavior will always help them improve and climb the corporate/business/success ladder faster.

When extrovert people are stressed out or are facing a crisis, they will feel that 'doubling-down' effect on how both aspects of their personalities need sex and need it now. Thankfully, because they respect themselves, if they are in a romantic relationship, these extroverts will initiate sex more frequently with their partners. They appreciate that sex will relieve their stress, and so they crave not only the intense acceptance that they receive while having sex, but they also crave the oxytocin release that follows every climax.

When introvert people are stressed out or are facing a crisis, they are pulled in opposite directions. On one hand, they need to focus on their career/project at hand.

Why it Works!
Maureen Pisani Ph.D.
www.ProThriveSBH.com

127

They are aware that they have a reputation to maintain, so completing the stressful project needs to get done and in fact, will get done. However, they also have that sexual tension building up. Because of their high levels of self-respect, these introverts, if in a relationship, will choose "quickies" over the elaborate sexual encounter their romantic partner prefers. If they are single, they usually have a" friends-with-benefits" arrangement where that person (usually an extrovert who is yearning for more sex) is at their beck and call for whenever they have the need. These people might even go as far as carving out enough time for masturbation to be possible, and then once the release was achieved, they return to the project, mentally putting in the extra minutes necessary to compensate for the time taken to climax. This way they achieve both – the completion of the project on time and stress relief.

- Low Levels of Self-Respect & *The Other F* -

This combination of traits creates people who function in a way to satisfy their sexual desires but couldn't care less about whom they have sex with or what repercussions their decisions could lead to.

This behavior is usually triggered in adolescence, when children are testing the waters and learning what their sexuality is and how their sexuality can influence their

Why it Works!
Maureen Pisani Ph.D.
www.ProThriveSBH.com

life. Sometimes, a bad experience, whether it was a painful or a negative sexual experience, where an adolescent ended up feeling used, and/or a secret sexual experience was shared publicly, and the individual was ridiculed - these incidents have marred these people's level of self-respect. It is truly a shame, because those old wounds are still affecting these individuals on a daily basis.

When life is going smoothly, people with this wiring still don't thrive. They have such a negative self-image that the best they can do is to function so minimally that they are constantly on the verge of disaster. These people have just enough money to survive this month, because working hard and saving would mean that they respect themselves, so that just doesn't happen. They will also behave in ways both personally and professionally that will ensure that others don't respect them either. Whether they procrastinate on the job or let people down, they will behave in ways where others don't see them in a positive light.

When extrovert people are facing a crisis or are stressed out and *The Other F* survival mechanism is triggered, these people basically have no choice but to have sex. They need to connect with another person in a way that offers that elusive acceptance, and sex will provide that for them.

Why it Works!
Maureen Pisani Ph.D.
www.ProThriveSBH.com

129

However, because of their low levels of self-respect, they will have sex with whomever is close by and available. Yes, these extroverts promise the other person that this is an easy, convenient hookup scenario. But afterwards, these extroverts are heartbroken, because their sexual partner (usually an introvert) just went along for the hookup and then walked away. This will reinforce to the extroverts that this is all they deserve.

When introvert people are stressed out or are facing a crisis, they have the pull to focus on their work, but inside, those low levels of self-respect intensify the need to postpone, procrastinate, and miss the deadline, because this will be in alignment with what they believe they deserve...nothing good to ever happen to them. While all this is happening, the buildup of sexual tension will be the perfect excuse to go have sex. If the introverts are in a relationship, they will initiate sex, but if single, then they will choose whomever is close by and available. If the stress continues to build, they will forego their desire for human connection and choose their tried-and-true system of masturbation. This way, they will spend time focusing on the sexual release, which will ensure that the project that is causing all the stress isn't completed. This way, they create the reality which aligns with their beliefs.

Why it Works!
Maureen Pisani Ph.D.
www.ProThriveSBH.com

SELF-LOVE

FIGHT

- High Levels of Self-Love and Fight -

This combination of traits creates people who do take action but who also value self-care and implement self-love in ways that enhance the quality of their life. These people's high levels of self-love mean that they will choose to eat right and exercise for the health benefits, they will ensure that their house is exactly how they had envisioned it would be, and they will work in an environment that is supportive, collaborative, and enjoyable. These people are go-getters, but they will intentionally pace themselves so that burnout doesn't occur.

This self-love is usually understated and never bragged about. However, when one observes intently, one can see how limits are self-imposed to enhance health, how hours of sleep are honored because they are incredibly appreciative of how important sleep is, and how certain foods and liquids are never ingested because they understand that what they eat, or drink will affect everything in their life.

When these individuals are facing a crisis, even though they know it's a bad situation, they will still come from this loving perspective.

Why it Works!
Maureen Pisani Ph.D.
www.ProThriveSBH.com

131

Yes, they will take action. Yes, they will take charge and handle and resolve it, but it will always be within the boundaries they deem to be appropriate and safe.

- Low Levels of Self-Love and Fight -

This combination of traits creates individuals who are go-getters but dislike themselves, sometimes to the point of self-hate. This internal dislike results in having these people work hard to advance, and then in the moment of truth, when the right people are there and it's the perfect opportunity to shine, these individuals will share something awful about themselves. They might share their worst attribute or describe themselves in a way that causes the "right people" to judge them negatively. This of course then ruins their possible advancement.

For low levels of self-love to be present, these people have had to have done things in the past of which they are not proud. They usually have a bumpy history, and those mistakes have resulted in these people judging themselves harshly.

These individuals usually find themselves in a contradictory situation. One part of them works really hard to improve and rise up in life, while the other part

Why it Works!
Maureen Pisani Ph.D.
www.ProThriveSBH.com

constantly denigrates and nullifies all that effort and work because internally, they know their deepest darkest secrets and therefore judge themselves for those actions constantly.

When stressed out or facing a crisis, these people will take action, but they will either do something that only minimally improves the crisis, or they will do the worst possible thing that will exacerbate the situation. This way, they've done something so their survival mechanism Fight has been assuaged, but the outcome is bad, which is in alignment with their low levels of self-love.

FLIGHT

- High Levels of Self-Love and Flight -

This combination of traits creates people who treat themselves with love in all ways, but if situations become uncomfortable, they will exit the scene, pronto.

These individuals know how to behave in ways that align with their personal standards of self-love. They will work and play hard, while also including self-care on a regular basis. But should a situation arise where behavior, conditions, or results are out of alignment with these people's levels of self-love, they will simply leave without explanation.

Why it Works!
Maureen Pisani Ph.D.
www.ProThriveSBH.com

133

On one hand, they understand how important taking care of oneself is. But if there's a situation that could possibly escalate to the point where they might be forced to speak up for themselves or take definitive action, these people's survival mechanism of "Flight" kicks in and they get out of there. They don't enjoy uncomfortable situations, and confrontation is high on that list, so leaving, quitting, walking away, and/or

ghosting someone will all be chosen before these people ever speak up for themselves or stand their ground.

- Low Levels of Self- Love and Flight -

This combination of traits creates individuals where self-destructive behavior and self-sabotage occur on a regular basis. These peoples' histories have trained them to see themselves as naughty, incorrigible, bad, unworthy, "damaged goods," "bad seed," even as despicable. These labels were heard so many times that these people ended up believing them. They truly identify with those awful labels, and so cannot find anything inside that's worth loving.

To make things worse, this negative behavior is repeated because their unconscious mind needs to stay within what it's gotten accustomed to.

Why it Works!
Maureen Pisani Ph.D.
www.ProThriveSBH.com

As soon as the negative behaviors build up to a crisis, these people walk away and escape even at the cost of ruining their reputation, because in these people's own opinion their reputation is already ruined.

FREEZE

- High levels of Self-Love and Freeze -

This combination of traits creates people who appreciate the true value of love. These individuals will love everyone around them and will go out of their way to help because they love the feeling of loving others. These people will also have a healthy standard of self-love where they will eat and drink wisely, where work-life balance is maintained, and where self-care is implemented regularly. These individuals understand that love is the currency that truly makes a difference.

However, if someone treats these people unkindly, or is rude to them, or they find themselves in a situation where harsh words need to be said, or a drastic decision needs to be taken, these people will freeze and not do anything.

There could also be the scenario where these people's high levels of self-love trigger the "freeze" response, because getting stressed will hurt them.

Why it Works!
Maureen Pisani Ph.D.
www.ProThriveSBH.com

135

Refusing to participate in the crisis and staying neutral seems to be more of a protective behavior than anything else.

This doesn't go well with the other parties involved in the crisis/situation. Usually, in a crisis or disagreement, "A" speaks to "B" and then "B" responds to "A." However, when "B" walks away or refuses to respond to "A," "A's" stress level and/or the severity of the situation, intensifies.

These individuals, who in this example would be "B," might internally wish to respond, but they will put themselves first. They will value their health, mental status, and peace of mind over everything else and the Freeze response is held onto, if not reinforced.

- Low Levels of Self-Love and Freeze -

This combination of traits creates people who have been brainwashed into believing that they aren't worthy of being loved. This is an incredibly painful place to live in, when one believes that they are so bad that being loved (one of the most basic requirements of life) is too good for them.

Why it Works!
Maureen Pisani Ph.D.
www.ProThriveSBH.com

This usually is instilled early on in life, where the child overhears/witnesses or is the primary receiver of awful abuse (emotional and verbal at the least, all the others possibly too). As children, each of us learns what the dynamics of the household are, and each of us adjusts our behavior to survive in whatever scenario is ruling the household.

If the house is positive, then adapting to being loved, accepted, cherished, and cared for is easy. However, if the family is dysfunctional where verbal, mental, and emotional abuse (at least) are a normal occurrence, that child grows up with a different set of beliefs than other children. That child, knowing that he/she has no other choice but to live in that house for a while, will acquiesce to the distorted truths that run amuck in the family. If the abuse continues, then that child will live their life believing what the abusive adults claim as their rationalizations, as truths.

This is the broken foundation on which that child will create their self-identity labels. If they hear how bad, unworthy, disappointing, _____ the child is, over and over for years, it truly isn't a surprise that that child will believe all those comments and own them as their truths.

Why it Works!
Maureen Pisani Ph.D.
www.ProThriveSBH.com

137

As an adult, people who have this kind of self-identity library cannot in all honesty think of themselves in a good way. The abuse went on for too long, which created too many negative imprints on their unconscious mind. The resultant reaction is to think so poorly of oneself that they might end up despising themselves. This is still occurring internally even when life is going smoothly.

When these people face a negative situation, a crisis, or anything that causes them stress, they will freeze, because over the years, not doing anything meant that they couldn't be judged or yelled at for doing the wrong thing. What these people don't understand is that as an adult, "Freezing" (not doing anything) is a response in and of itself.

These individuals will not and cannot function when stress levels are high, because they can't risk triggering all that abusive behavior again. Remember, that these individuals' primary response to stress is with a life-or-death intensity. They would rather receive the verbal backlash from the others in the situation than risk doing the wrong thing.

Why it Works!
Maureen Pisani Ph.D.
www.ProThriveSBH.com

Even if the others' response is harsh or unfair, because of these people's low levels of self-love, they will stay, won't leave, won't respond, because they believe that they deserve the horrendous outcome or repercussions their freezing created.

FOOD

- High Levels of Self-Love and Food -

This combination of traits creates individuals who value loving and being loved. These people are also aware that each of us is in charge of creating our own happiness, so they have high levels of Self-Love. This translates into behaviors and patterns of thinking where decisions being made according to how in alignment to their levels of Self-love these behaviors are.

These people treat themselves with kindness and love, always ensuring that they are having a good day and that their thinking is positive. Their emotions are optimistic and loving to themselves and others.

When life is going smoothly, these people will choose foods that will not only maintain their levels of health but increase them. These individuals are usually aware of the benefits of specific foods and even food

Why it Works!
Maureen Pisani Ph.D.
www.ProThriveSBH.com

139

combinations, where some foods become more potent if this or that supplement is added. They are committed to making their life better one decision at a time, and that includes food choices and volumes ingested.

When these people face a crisis or are stressed out, and their survival mechanism is triggered, they will indulge in food, but it will be within reason. They might admit to overdoing it and will chastise themselves for losing control and potentially undermining months of good eating choices. However, if asked how they lost control, it will be a surprisingly mild offense. These people might lose control and eat one doughnut; but because they normally stay away from wheat and sugar on good days, having that one doughnut breaks all kinds of rules for them. The fact that they are aware and usually stick to healthy and beneficial choices, the eating of that one doughnut can still create havoc in these people's systems. Their physiology is so clean that ingesting that single doughnut could trigger all the blood sugar rollercoasters previously mentioned.

- Low Levels of Self-Love and Food -

This combination of traits creates individuals who don't love who they truly are.

Why it Works!
Maureen Pisani Ph.D.
www.ProThriveSBH.com

Yes, these people could possibly fake liking themselves in public to maintain the pseudo-appearance of normalcy; but they in fact are the only one who knows the 100% truth about themselves. And truth be told, they don't love who they are at all.

This is usually a trait that begins in childhood. This is a time when most of us are exposed to new situations, and we're either given the wrong information from the get-go, or we come to erroneous conclusions because as children, we don't have a fully developed brain yet. As children, we tend to accept what we observe and hear as fact, so if a family friend who has high levels of self-love is seen as conceited or their behavior is seen as self-absorbed, then as children we might simply categorize self-love as a bad thing, thinking that if we did opposite of what that family friend did, we'd be loved more.

Another situation is that as children, these people were verbally and emotionally abused and horrible things were said to them, which they believed and internalized. They went through life with these awful comments as truths, and so now behave in a way that is congruent with their internal beliefs.

Another possibility is that while growing up, these people saw their parents' behavior and accepted it as the right behavior to replicate.

Why it Works!
Maureen Pisani Ph.D.
www.ProThriveSBH.com

141

However, if these individuals' parents had low levels of self-love, that's what these people have been practicing throughout their life without fully understanding why they never really felt good.

The replication of the negative behavior reinforced belonging to the family unit, which overrode all the potential consequences. It was more important to them to belong and behave exactly how either or both parents behaved, than to worry about how their behavior affected their life.

When these people are facing a crisis or are stressed out, they will only focus on satisfying the immediate need to diminish the stress: to eat whatever will soothe the fastest, which is usually the worst possible choice available. These people's low level of self-love will never send any red flags to make them pause and ponder a decision. When they want to self-soothe, they will… with whatever is available.

Although these people will go to the doctor and maybe get regular checkups, they don't do it for themselves, but to stop everybody around them from pestering them to get things checked.

Why it Works!
Maureen Pisani Ph.D.
www.ProThriveSBH.com

These people are usually noncompliant for the simple fact that if they did follow doctor's orders, they would feel better and their health might improve, and that's in conflict with how they think of themselves.

THE OTHER F

- High Levels of Self-Love and *The Other F*
-

This combination of traits creates people who love themselves and love the fact that other people love them too! These people's lives pivot on their self-love behavior. Everything they do has been assessed and deemed appropriate for them to implement. Whether it's personal or professional, everything these people do will be within the range of behavior that's in alignment with their high levels of self-love.

When life is going smoothly, these people thrive. They make sure that their work environment, their family, and their friends are all positive, supportive, and loving. These people live life with a "share-the-wealth" mentality. When they're happy, they do things for others around them to make others happy too. These individuals not only rise in life, but also help others to rise.

Why it Works!
Maureen Pisani Ph.D.
www.ProThriveSBH.com

143

However, when the extrovert people face a crisis or are stressed out, even though they have high levels of self-love, their *Other F* survival mechanism is still triggered. They are intensely aware of the sexual yearning but are always incredibly aware that unwise choices have the potential to be damaging to them and their reputation.

Extrovert people with this wiring, if in a relationship, will definitely have sex with their romantic partners because this way, they achieve success in both departments. They achieve the oxytocin release which reduces the stress, and their behavior is well within their levels of self-love.

When the introvert people face a crisis and are stressed out, their first instinct is to see what they can do to handle the situation themselves. Introverts fear losing control, so if they're in charge of the crisis, they might be able to resolve it and minimize the potential damage. But, as they're dealing with the crisis, they are distracted by their sexual buildup. To them, it's an annoyance, but they know that at some point they will have to deal with it. Most introverts with high levels of self-love will calculate a risk-benefit ratio to see if/when it will be a suitable time to switch their focus from the project to deal with this annoying sexual need.

Why it Works!
Maureen Pisani Ph.D.
www.ProThriveSBH.com

Most will postpone the sexual release, but if the buildup is too distracting, even the introvert people will succumb to having sex, or at least masturbating to reduce that sexual intensity. These sexual encounters will be quick, functional, and basically as impersonal as possible. Once release has been achieved, then they can return to dealing with the crisis and give it their undivided attention.

- Low Levels of Self-Love and *The Other F* -

This combination of traits creates people who believe that there's nothing in them that's worth loving. These low levels of self-love could have been triggered at any point in their past. It could have been that in childhood, they heard their parents complain about them, or that their mother bragged about having been a "career woman until the babies came along." These people might have been spoken to so harshly and abusively that they just believe all those horrible things they were told. It could also have been triggered at the end of a relationship, where their ex lashed out and said things to intentionally hurt them. Regardless of where it stems from, these people believe that they don't deserve to be loved.

Why it Works!
Maureen Pisani Ph.D.
www.ProThriveSBH.com

145

When life is going smoothly, these people will not choose wisely. Whether it's the food they're eating, the people they're spending time with, or the job they have, these individuals barely survive. Their thoughts, decisions and actions are based on self-sabotage, because it's unthinkable to them to succeed. Even when they claim to be doing their best, at some point something's going to happen, because for them, the life they need to live has to be in alignment with their low levels of self-love.

When extrovert people are facing a crisis or are stressed out and *The Other F* survival mechanism is triggered, these people ignore doing anything about the crisis and go out on the prowl to have sex. They don't have a fully thought-out strategy, just that undeniable urge that they need to have sexual intercourse as soon as possible. This urgency overrides any pausing to assess who the potential sexual partner is, so the wrong people are chosen. Having sex only temporarily relieves the stressor, because as soon as the wave of oxytocin has passed, all the extrovert is left with is the disappointment of the encounter, because the sexual partner (usually an introvert) just up and left them, right there. As the disappointment settles in, these people tend to feel worse, but feeling worse and recognizing their bad choices falls in alignment with their low levels of self-love.

Why it Works!
Maureen Pisani Ph.D.
www.ProThriveSBH.com

When introvert people are stressed out or are facing a crisis, their initial priority is to focus on the stressor, especially if it is a work project and a deadline is coming up. Introverts see their career as their top priority; however, their low levels of self-love undermine their motivation because they will self-sabotage every chance they get. Introverts are aware that they might not make the deadline, which intensifies the stress levels, and *The Other F* survival mechanism is triggered.

Initially they will do their best to ignore the sexual tension. They will focus on the project, but they will reach the tipping point where satisfying their sexual need falls in alignment with their unconscious need to not succeed. Their low levels of self-love create the scenario where having sex causes them to fail professionally.

If the introvert people are in a relationship, they might choose the person they are in a committed relationship with to have sex, or they might choose whomever is around and available. As mentioned previously, introverts discriminate between sex and love, so for them having sex is a means to an end. In this case, even though having sex offers sexual release, sex is actually chosen as a distraction to avoid focusing on the crisis.

Why it Works!
Maureen Pisani Ph.D.
www.ProThriveSBH.com

147

CHAPTER 6

HOW DOES ONE RESET TO SAFE ?

We face stressors constantly as we go through life. Most are the daily stressors we have gotten accustomed to – freeway traffic, dealing with family, dealing with the children, negotiating with all the different personalities at work, working overtime to meet a deadline, having too much month at the end of the money (Jim Rohn), etc. These usual stressors affect us in ways we don't even realize. We think of them as mostly background noise, but they are still triggering the Sympathetic Nervous System, which in turn triggers the survival mechanisms within us.

When the sympathetic nervous system is triggered, adrenaline and cortisol are released into our system to help us have that surge of energy that we would need IF we were facing a hungry saber-tooth tiger. However, we are facing deadlines, meetings, tough customers, defiant teenagers, oblivious spouses, and/or never-ending bills, not life-threatening scenarios. Our body doesn't differentiate that the stressors we face nowadays aren't threatening our lives.

Our body, and therefore we, are still experiencing that flood of adrenaline and cortisol.

Why it Works!
Maureen Pisani Ph.D.
www.ProThriveSBH.com

We still respond according to which survival mechanism was triggered. It still takes time for us to metabolize the stress hormones and attempt to reset to safe. However, because these background stressors happen continuously and repeatedly during our day, consecutive waves of adrenaline and cortisol are released into our body, which means that our physiology is in constant survival mode.

Having the sympathetic nervous system engaged long-term plays havoc with our physiology and with our health. That's when blood pressure rises and stays elevated, and when sleep issues begin. How is one supposed to sleep deeply and let go of the day, when all one can think about is what happened during the day, how it's going to affect everything, and does one have the capability to solve the problem? Lack of sleep, both types of insomnia and disturbed sleep when nightmares occur, all have a significant effect on the physiology.

Then, when something serious happens – a negative diagnosis, a horrible car crash, a death in the family, a loss of a job, a global pandemic - then the flood gates are opened, and we have such a huge release of those hormones that our body overreacts.

Why it Works!
Maureen Pisani Ph.D.
www.ProThriveSBH.com

149

So, resetting to SAFE, re-triggering the Parasympathetic nervous system, will interrupt the cascading negative effects, not to mention all the benefits that empowerment brings.

One of the questions that I'm asked the most is, "How do YOU deal with stress?" Well, there are few things that I do, and yes, I will be sharing them with you.

I am intensely aware of how we – you, me, all of us - react when we're stressed out. We lose our ability to reason, think, assess, gauge, make decisions, or act cognitively, where actions end up being reactive instead of pro-active.

When we drop down to our Primitive Mind, we become reactive and harsh words are said (words that can never be taken back), intense reactions, decisions and actions happen (that we will regret afterwards but can never remedy), and we function just like our Neanderthal ancestors would have. That is a big shame, because we as a species have evolved. Our brains now have a Pre-Frontal Cortex which enables us to function in a more comprehensive way. This pre-frontal cortex, otherwise known as the "adult brain" oversees the filtering of what our reptilian brain suggests as appropriate retaliation.

Why it Works!
Maureen Pisani Ph.D.
www.ProThriveSBH.com

I always use this example to share how the pre-frontal cortex works. My Dad was a true gentleman. While driving, he would yell out "You bloomin' basket" to anyone who cut him off. Now, with little children in the car he might have thought the words "you bloody bastard," BUT he verbalized "you bloomin' basket." This way he had his response, but it was in alignment with him being a great Dad and not scandalizing his children with his choice of crude words. Dad's pre-frontal cortex had intervened and amended his words to make them more appropriate for the surroundings he was in.

If we were to fly off the handle every time something went wrong and our stress levels increased, that constant triggering of our survival mechanisms would play havoc on our health. Personally, I'd much rather take a moment, pause, take a breath, assess the situation, and then make an educated decision. Yes, I can do all that without my blood pressure spiking, without my muscles cramping and without stressing my heart. Fair? I tend to think that we all deserve to give ourselves that pause. Don't you?

Being able to intentionally reset to "calm and safe" works wonders on our physiology, not to mention how empowered we become when we know what to do whenever things get out of hand.

Why it Works!
Maureen Pisani Ph.D.
www.ProThriveSBH.com

151

I appreciate that some have a more delicate constitution and/or have had a more traumatic history and are susceptible to higher levels of anxiety and panic attacks. These techniques will help you, too.

My sole intention is to offer you tried-and-true techniques that will stop the escalation of the stress, and reinforce the notion that yes, you can put the crisis on hold. You have the tools to help you overcome, conquer, win, and emerge as triumphant.

As you now know, stress is everything and anything that our conscious mind feels is just too much, too difficult, too shocking, or simply put, too overwhelming. As soon as we feel that we're out of our depth, we're stressed out. This is when systems go berserk, and we feel the effects of stress. We usually feel like we're losing control or we're going out of control. That's when anxiety and/or panic attacks strike. Having tools to utilize in that moment will immediately increase empowerment, enhance your self-identity, and minimize (if not remove completely) your prior responses and experiences.

Here are a few techniques that I've implemented myself and have taught countless clients to do. These techniques are easy to learn and practice, and yet are very effective.

Why it Works!
Maureen Pisani Ph.D.
www.ProThriveSBH.com

If you feel better having them written down on flash cards, do so. You can have them in your phone, or you can share these tips with the people with whom you interact the most, so that in a moment of crisis, they can remind you to utilize them.

1. YOU CONTROL YOUR RESPONSE.

The first thing is to remember that sentence *"The only thing you can control is your response to the situation."* I have found this to be incredibly true. In our lives we are aware that we control several things, but we are also aware that there are innumerable scenarios where we do not have total control. As you now know, simply reacting affects us in horrible ways, so choosing our response is how we get to be happy and ultimately healthy.

Let's use driving as an example. Yes, I'm in charge of my car and my driving, but I'm not in charge of all the other drivers and cars that are on the freeway with me. So, if a car speeds past me and cuts me off, instead of screaming at the

Why it Works!
Maureen Pisani Ph.D.
www.ProThriveSBH.com

153

other driver, which would affect my health negatively, I think of scenarios that will trigger an acceptable response within me. If I'm looking to trigger compassion, I might think, "Ooh they must be late for an important appointment." I might actually think of that scene from *Alice in Wonderland* where the words "I'm late, I'm late for a very important date," are sung in my head. Then I wish them a safe drive, hoping that they arrive on time. And then I let it go. However,

if I'm looking to trigger some humor, I might think "Ooh, they're in desperate need of a bathroom and the situation's getting dire!" and then I find myself smiling and chuckling and it's over. I've let it go completely.

This way you can see how I'm aware of the crazy drivers around me. But instead of letting it affect me, thereby ruining my mood and possibly harming my physiology, I am in charge of my response. I intentionally choose to respond with compassion or humor.

This is truly an effective technique. Prepare these scenarios in your head, so when it happens, you instantly bring up one of the pre-planned

Why it Works!
Maureen Pisani Ph.D.
www.ProThriveSBH.com

scripts, which will trigger positive responses within you and help you stay calm and relaxed. The more you practice this, the easier it will be to enjoy the healthy benefits of being calm and happy.

2. SAY 5 BIG NUMBERS OUT OF SEQUENCE.

This technique is amazingly easy and incredibly effective. When things are spiraling and you feel yourself losing control, where the tears are starting to well up, where the heart is pounding, the hands are sweating, and you can't quite catch your breath... STOP. PAUSE. AND SAY 5 BIG NUMBERS OUT OF SEQUENCE.

This is a tried-and-true way to retrigger your parasympathetic nervous system and reset to safe and calm in a short period of time. Here's why it works. We know that our brains are split into two hemispheres, where the Right hemisphere specializes in Emotions, Creativity, Relationships and Symbolism, and the Left hemisphere specializes in Linear and Logical thinking, Career, and Finances.

Why it Works!
Maureen Pisani Ph.D.
www.ProThriveSBH.com

155

As the person's stress level is escalating and the panic attack symptomology has begun, that's when that individual's Right hemisphere is in overdrive. Stopping and saying five big numbers out of sequence – 4,483, to 2,031, to 9,627, to 1,853, to 7,238 - will cause the Left hemisphere to go into hyperactivity. As soon as the Left hemisphere goes into overdrive, the Right hemisphere (where all the emotions reside) is forced to go into hypoactivity and begins to settle down. Most people find that one round of numbers calms things down significantly. However, if more rounds are needed, this is an easy enough technique to implement. Once that happens, the panic attack is over, and you're back in complete control.

In over 16 years of practice, the worst panic attack I helped with required 5 rounds before the lady was completely settled down, calm, peaceful and back to being fully composed. This technique works like a charm.

3. ASK FOR A TIGHT HUG.

When one's anxiety is intensifying, and one is feeling on the verge of spinning out, asking for a tight hug will help.

Why it Works!
Maureen Pisani Ph.D.
www.ProThriveSBH.com

When you're being hugged, apart from the acceptance it translates to for the extroverts, hugging tight also allows for the body to release oxytocin. This hormone is known to reduce anxiety and enhance relaxation, which in turn creates several beneficial physiological responses like lowering the heart rate and the blood pressure.

However, if you experience anxiety and panic attacks on a regular basis, investing in a back brace will help. Back braces are adjustable, and one is completely in charge of how high and how tight these braces are worn. Yes, you can wear the back brace around your torso over your underwear and under your clothes. You can wear it all day and all night long if it helps calm things down inside. This way you'll feel safe and calm, no one knows that you're wearing it, and you'll feel the empowerment. [We have 'thunder-vests' for our pets which we know calm them down significantly.]

My intention is to offer you techniques that (i) will help you deal with and overcome the stress and (ii) work.

Why it Works!
Maureen Pisani Ph.D.
www.ProThriveSBH.com

157

4. STOP, BREATHE IN AND OUT FORCEFULLY.

When we are stressed, panicked, or spinning out, our breathing is usually brief and shallow. We usually breathe using only the apices of the lungs, which is an incredibly inefficient way to breathe. When we shallow breathe, we are also reinforcing that "I can't catch my breath" scenario that can lead to a full-blown panic attack. Stopping, breathing in deeply and exhaling forcefully will trigger our Parasympathetic system, which re-sets our physiology to SAFE.

Again, this is something you can utilize anywhere, anytime, with anyone. We all breathe, so just breathing in and exhaling forcefully will instantly send a wave of calmness through your system which will help you get back in full control.

Why it Works!
Maureen Pisani Ph.D.
www.ProThriveSBH.com

5. EAT PROTEIN EVERY 3 HOURS.

Our bodies are a fuel burning machine. That fuel comes from what we eat and what we have stored as fat. What we eat is usually broken down into carbohydrates, fat, and protein. The carbohydrates are broken down into sugars which the body needs. (The brain needs about ½ teaspoon of sugar constantly to function at its best.) However, overindulging in carbohydrates and sugars initially launches a spike in the blood sugar levels, which is what happens when the children rev up from what we call a "sugar rush." However, we've also seen what happens once their bodies metabolize all that sugar. We've seen children fall asleep standing, with their head on the couch and they are out cold.

All those changes happen within us. However, as adults we don't outwardly rev up and we certainly can't pass out cold and fall asleep when our blood sugar drops. We need to stay awake and continue on with our life.

Here's what happens physiologically when life is going smoothly. Once we've eaten too many carbohydrates and/or sugars for lunch, our blood sugar level spikes. This causes the pancreas to secrete enough insulin to bring that blood sugar level down to within normal limits.

Why it Works!
Maureen Pisani Ph.D.
www.ProThriveSBH.com

159

Once it's back down, then we experience that 3 PM slump. As soon as that happens and there's not enough sugar in the blood, we either eat or drink more, or our system releases Adrenaline and Cortisol to keep the system going. However, if we are

stressed, the amount of food we think is enough is burned through faster, which leads to repeated blood sugar drops. This inadvertently leads to the body's sympathetic nervous system being triggered, which releases of adrenaline and cortisol. These hormones are amplifiers – so if you're happy, you'll be happier; but if you're stressed, worried, upset, or anxious, these hormones will intensify all these to frantic and panicked.

There are some who when worried or stressed don't eat, and this just exacerbates the scenario. There are some whose normal routine is to skip breakfast. This leads to that individual not having ingested anything for over 10, 11, or 12 hours! Their body still needs fuel, but because this individual is not eating, their bodies are

Why it Works!
Maureen Pisani Ph.D.
www.ProThriveSBH.com

forced to release the hormones just to keep the systems going. Once they do eat, they usually overeat because they're hungry and after 12 hours, most anyone would be hungry. And another vicious cycle is launched.

As all this is happening, these individuals with what's known as "Irregular Blood Sugars" have symptoms that just make their day worse. Irregular blood sugar levels create havoc internally, which usually show up as emotional overreactions, intensified PMS symptoms, intense irritability, inexplicable forgetfulness, lack of mental focus, lethargy, emotional apathy, horrible sleep patterns, and out of control panic attacks. The panic attacks are labelled as "a psychological response to a physiological trigger".
This can all be amended through a simple change in these people's lifestyle. It will be the easiest thing they've ever done, and it will also be the most boring thing they've ever done... BUT IT WORKS.

As soon as the pattern is noticed, when life is going smoothly, these people need to ingest protein every 3 hours, to keep a regulated blood sugar level.

Why it Works!
Maureen Pisani Ph.D.
www.ProThriveSBH.com

161

When they are facing a crisis, or are stressed out, these individuals need to ingest protein every 2 hours, to keep their blood sugar levels stable. If we prevent the first domino from falling... nothing else will happen. Maintaining a regulated blood sugar level keeps the body safe, where the sympathetic nervous system is not triggered. This is when and how the physical body will stay SAFE.

For these people, it is highly recommended to have breakfast, a snack, lunch, a snack, dinner, and a snack throughout their waking hours. If there's too much time between the last snack and bedtime, the individual can have either a couple of slices of turkey or a teaspoon of peanut butter, as both have protein and tryptophan which will satisfy the protein requirements for the body. The tryptophan will help the person sleep better too. This is not a situation where there needs to be a banquet eaten at every sitting. Protein is in everything. Yes, you can have animal protein, but there are countless options for vegetable protein too. The best advice I can give you is to PREPARE.

Why it Works!
Maureen Pisani Ph.D.
www.ProThriveSBH.com

Once all the snacks are prepared and are in the fridge, a cooler, your bag, or in your car...every time your alarm goes off (120-180 minutes), you can simply eat/drink your pre-planned protein and your body will continue functioning within its healthy boundaries.

In a few days (I always recommend giving it at least 21 days), people notice a calmer disposition, having more energy and a more positive outlook on life. They feel more like themselves, they are more in control, and all those negative experiences and episodes have diminished, if not stopped altogether. They are more resilient, more focused, and their body feels safe again. This transformation is great to experience, and as their hypnotherapist, incredible to observe.

6. THE BOWENWORK RE-SET TO SAFE.

I am blessed to know Sharon Edmiston, an Advanced Certified Bowenwork Practitioner who has been in private practice for over 10 years. Bowenwork for healing re-sets the body to begin healing permanently.

Why it Works!
Maureen Pisani Ph.D.
www.ProThriveSBH.com

163

Bowenwork realigns the body by making small, rolling movements over ligaments, soft tissue, tendons, and muscles. This is done at precise points on the body, using gentle pressure. It works both in person and long-distance. If you would like additional information, just visit Sharon's website – www.BowenworkforHealing.com.

I have had the privilege to work with Sharon and have received incredible results.

If you are in a situation where the stress is escalating, and you need to do something right now to calm down and re-set to safe, here's the Bowenwork exercise I have utilized and have taught clients to do.

Place both sets of fingertips on the xyphoid process, which is the cartilage along the midline where your ribs meet. It's where the solar plexus is. This exercise entails taking three deep breaths. You will move your fingertips only on the exhales.

Why it Works!
Maureen Pisani Ph.D.
www.ProThriveSBH.com

Following the first deep inhale, as you're exhaling slowly, you will slide your right fingertips along the right ribs, going from the midline to the side of the waist on the right.
Bring the hand back to midline.

Following the second deep inhale, as you're exhaling slowly, you will slide your left fingertips along the left ribs, going from the midline to the side of the waist on the left.
Bring the hand back to midline.

Following the third deep inhale, as you're exhaling slowly, slide both sets of fingertips along the midline halfway from the xyphoid to the navel.

This exercise might take you approximately 15 seconds, but you will notice an internal shift occurring inside. If after a few minutes, you'd like to intensify the re-set to SAFE, repeat the exercise.
Yes, knowing about this exercise and practicing it is empowering you. The more techniques you know, the more empowered you are.

Why it Works!
Maureen Pisani Ph.D.
www.ProThriveSBH.com

165

CHAPTER 7

HOW DOES HYPNOTHERAPY HELP ?

I have found Hypnotherapy to be an incredible modality to install, adjust, or remove behaviors. Yes, the client has to desire these upgrades. Yes, I describe my sessions as "mental collaboration." Yes, the upgrades that the clients have requested, planned, and strategized as to why they will be better off living a 2.0 version of themselves were implemented and became theirs.

I'm thankful for every single client that I've had the honor to serve. Each of them has gifted me with something – whether it was seeing life from their perspective, observing the incredible levels of love that they shared, getting my mind to create new pathways for them to live a better today, every day; watching them evolve, sharing their successes or grief, each of them touched my heart. Their individuality made me think, adapt, adjust, and personalize everything I thought of to their needs, their perceptions, their language patterns, their self-identity levels, and their safety levels, which in turn gifted me the opportunity to improve my skill. For that I'll be eternally grateful to each of them.

As I've mentioned before, I believe in empowering my clients both cognitively and hypnotically.

Why it Works!
Maureen Pisani Ph.D.
www.ProThriveSBH.com

When there are events, incidents, or memories that are undermining what the clients are working towards, upgrading their unconscious minds through hypnotherapy has offered phenomenal results.

Through Hypnotherapy, upgrades are accepted and implemented into the individual's daily life. These results become innate to them where their behavior, reaction, or response is different from their past behavior, but simultaneously feels natural, too.

Here are a few techniques that I have utilized in my practice.

1. HOW TO RELEASE PAST TRAUMAS

Individuals have traumatic experiences in life. When trauma occurs, the Amygdala in the brain, the part that recognizes when we are safe or in danger, goes into high alert, which triggers the sympathetic nervous system. It sends a message down to the adrenals that release adrenaline and cortisol. This launches the body into its survival mechanism.

As soon as this occurs, the Hippocampus, which oversees the filing of memories, stops functioning. This creates a situation where that traumatic event is remembered and re-experienced as a current event and therefore re-lived in the moment (happening right now, right here) repeatedly and without warning.

Why it Works!
Maureen Pisani Ph.D.
www.ProThriveSBH.com

167

The amygdala is constantly on the alert. It's what keeps us feeling safe, so once a trauma occurs, and the amygdala triggers the sympathetic nervous system which sends the entire body into survival mode. However, after the trauma is over, the amygdala is still on the alert for whatever might be deemed unsafe, so if anything resembles that original trauma or a portion of it, the amygdala will respond instantly and the whole cycle is relaunched. This is not only traumatic for the person, but also makes that person feel incredibly uncertain of themselves and of their lives. This is what is generally known as Post Traumatic Stress Disorder (P.T.S.D.).

The amygdala's function and our hippocampal function are beneath our awareness, so most don't think that there's much one can do. However, hypnotherapy accesses the unconscious mind that is also beneath our awareness.

Over the years, I have helped countless people who came in either with an official P.T.S.D. diagnosis, or because it was a personal traumatic experience that the client didn't think of it as P.T.S.D. These techniques have helped.

We know that the unconscious mind will implement suggestions that are within the client's morals, ethics, and beliefs.

Why it Works!
Maureen Pisani Ph.D.
www.ProThriveSBH.com

It will also accept and implement suggestions that the client deems acceptable and safe. During the cognitive portion of the session, I go over the trauma (so later I can inform the unconscious mind that the client had released the trauma verbally), and then I walk the client through how their life will be when these haphazard debilitating experiences stop.

If the client is stuck and cannot imagine a future that is calm, where they are completely empowered, then I'm aware that there are secondary gain issues that have to be worked on before the client can release it. Sometimes, it's also the situation that the client's unnerving response – heart palpitations, crying, shaking muscles, reliving the experience in the moment, and more - have shaken this person to their core and they are so broken that they don't recognize themselves anymore. In that case, it's not a secondary gains situation, but a rebuilding of the original person back to being strong, in charge, in control, where they can depend on themselves, on their body and their mind, completely once again.

When neither of those scenarios is present, and the client can visualize and imagine what their happy, successful, free, independent, and reliable future will be…then they are ready for the upgrade.

Why it Works!
Maureen Pisani Ph.D.
www.ProThriveSBH.com

169

Once in a hypnotic state, I walk them through a visualization that will help them through re-organizing their memories and filing all the negative memories all the way back.

[The full script is my Timeless Hypnotic Scripts II, Titled 'Recesses of Your Mind' (#20)]

I walk the client through seeing how their memories have become all jumbled up. They need to acknowledge what the current situation is, then how they can watch their memories be re-organized, but I also have them file all their negative memories behind all the positive memories.

Over the years, I have utilized the full script for the first session. However, during follow-up sessions, I utilize a more succinct version to keep filing any and all negative memories to the distant past. I've chosen to have them filed to the day the client was three years, three months, and three days old.

I've chosen that specific day for a couple of reasons: (i) very rarely do we have conscious memories from that age, so when the unconscious mind links those negative memories to that day, their usually gone and forgotten, and (ii) 333 is the most mystic of numbers, so as I, Maureen (mere mortal) am helping them, I'm also invoking the highest of powers to bless them into a better tomorrow.

Why it Works!
Maureen Pisani Ph.D.
www.ProThriveSBH.com

As part of my regular practice, I record the hypnotic portion and email it to the client. Their homework is to listen to the recording every evening as they're falling asleep. This re-listening reinforces the suggestions and within a short period of time, the implementation of the re-filing of the memories is so complete, that clients will forget to mention the trauma, or come in to discuss different issues.

2. HOW TO RE-SET TO SAFE - HYPNOTICALLY.

Some people live life feeling safe everywhere, all the time, with everyone. Others aren't so lucky. Some individuals have had such traumatic events, and have done their best to overcome them, but the resultant lifestyle is that they just don't feel safe any longer. These individuals go through routines every evening to ensure that they are safe, but the slightest of situations retriggers their amygdala to set off their sympathetic nervous system and the cycle continues.

What we have here, is that these people have been through so much that their mind is constantly looking for the proverbial red flags, because as soon as they notice a red flag, they can take action, meaning they will never be caught unaware again.

Why it Works!
Maureen Pisani Ph.D.
www.ProThriveSBH.com

171

Taking action to these people means ensuring safety. However, when they are completely focused on looking out for these red flags, they tend to miss all the green flags. These green flags are all the signs and evidence that these people are safe.

Because danger can mean a potential life-or-death situation, people who have experienced repeated trauma will tend to be hypervigilant even in scenarios and situations where everyone else is relaxed, having fun, and feeling safe.

Please keep in mind that these individuals are deadly serious about how unsafe they feel, and this constant state of "being on edge" wreaks havoc with their system. Some even reach the point that regardless of what they are observing, their mind is still on the alert for the "just in case" situation.

The best way to start the journey to safety is to teach these people how to take one step at a time, where each step is solid fact. And, yes, there is a way to start this. Our physiology will always let us know how we're truly feeling. When we feel safe internally, our heart beat is rhythmic – slow and steady; our breathing is deep and rhythmic, where we are breathing from the bases of our lungs; and our muscles (especially our trapezius, lumbar, and TMJ muscles) are relaxed.

Why it Works!
Maureen Pisani Ph.D.
www.ProThriveSBH.com

When the clients confirm that their body is functioning like this, then they have facts to confirm that their own body IS SAFE. This awareness is something they can depend on. I then walk them through a long list of places and scenarios that they experience either daily or regularly and ask them if in "_____" scenario, do they feel safe. I always ask. I never assume, because even though I understand that the clients have shared a lot with me, there might be situations I am unaware of, and assuming and pre-determining that that space, that location, or that person is safe, but for them isn't, will unravel the entire thing. So, I ask about each possible situation and they answer and only after they confirm that to them taking a shower is safe, standing at the kitchen sink is safe, washing the dishes is safe, sitting on the couch is safe, sleeping in their own bed is safe, sitting in the driver's seat of their car is safe, sitting at their desk in the office is safe, etc. I build a long, detailed list, putting in every single scenario we can think of together.

Then, once they're in a hypnotic state, I first take them through a slow and thorough progressive relaxation, ensuring that they are in a deep state of comfort. Then I ask them to confirm that they are relaxed and feeling safe.

Why it Works!
Maureen Pisani Ph.D.
www.ProThriveSBH.com

173

Once that is established, I go through the entire list, reinforcing that they acknowledged that when they are in that location, they are safe. To engage both brains, thereby making these suggestions acceptable to both hemispheres, I alternate from saying "Safe" to "S-A-F-E." When I say "safe" as a word, the right hemisphere receives it, so the emotional attachment to the situation has been handled. Being that the right hemisphere also specializes in creativity, it's in charge of allowing all these suggestions to be implemented to new situations and new scenarios. When I say "S-A-F-E," and spell it out, I'm engaging the left hemisphere, which specializes in linear and logical thinking. So, when I state that the client has acknowledged and approved that sitting at their desk is safe, the left hemisphere will accept and implement the suggestion, because it just makes sense.

I also encourage the client to become aware of any other situations or scenarios they find themselves in, and with full intention, check their physiology to confirm that they are in fact safe there too.

Why it Works!
Maureen Pisani Ph.D.
www.ProThriveSBH.com

3. HOW TO PRE-DETERMINE BEHAVIORS.

The biggest issue clients have is that after their history of over-responding to the traumatic memory, they are afraid that they won't know how to stay in control when something else triggers their sympathetic nervous system.

They know that other individuals have different responses according to the different situations they face, but internally, these people feel like they go from 0 60, completely losing control, in a split second. It's a behavior they would like to discontinue but have no idea how.

Remember, that as soon as the brain comes up with a behavior that it deems to be protective of the individual, it will keep responding in the same way, regardless of how intense or mild the situation is. If the amygdala feels threatened, it's launching every response at 100%. That behavior will continue to be relaunched until the programming in the unconscious mind is amended. Yes, Hypnotherapy is an outstanding modality for this, as it gives the best results to the smallest efforts. All that person has to do is re-listen to the recording to keep strengthening the suggestions that will solidify the new response.

Why it Works!
Maureen Pisani Ph.D.
www.ProThriveSBH.com

175

Over the years, we have all had behaviors and habits that we outgrew. It's a natural process. As babies, we sucked our thumbs, but we don't anymore. As toddlers we drank from a sippy cup, but we don't anymore. As children we cried and threw tantrums, we don't anymore. As adolescents we had certain behaviors that we outgrew, so we don't do those behaviors any longer. As we grow up, as a human being, we naturally outgrow behaviors.

Being that this outgrowing behavior is a natural phenomenon and a fact, I can utilize it. Even though it is incredibly capable of creating fantasy and fiction, the unconscious mind needs a foundation based on facts when dealing with therapeutic upgrades.

As the client is receiving all the hypnotic suggestions, starting with facts, where the client's unconscious mind is agreeing, I'm building an unconscious "yes set." When I share with the client's unconscious mind that they once were tremendously attached to their blankey as a baby but outgrew that attachment, the client will internally agree. When I mention that once they sat in a highchair as a toddler, but outgrew that highchair, and now are incredibly comfortable sitting in a regular chair, they agree.

Why it Works!
Maureen Pisani Ph.D.
www.ProThriveSBH.com

When I mention that as a child they threw tantrums, but they outgrew that behavior, they agree. Then, once I have the client and their unconscious mind agreeing with me on their own factual history, then I can continue extrapolating into how they are outgrowing these current situations.

During this process, I include how outgrowing all those previous behaviors allowed them to learn and implement new behaviors that were much more beneficial for them. They agree. Then I start guiding them through how the new behaviors will be. I never mention the negative behavior they are looking to release. I just call it "the old negative behavior."

Suggestions will be given like this: *"instead of that old negative behavior, when you find yourself in this situation (and I describe it), you will connect with feeling calm, peaceful, relaxed and safe. It will be quite acceptable for you to be calm, where conversations are easy, where you are completely in control, where your heartbeat, your pulse, your breathing rate are all within normal limits and stay within normal limits. You will notice that this response is more comfortable and enjoyable than you had originally hoped for, and you like it so much that you make it permanently yours."*

Why it Works!
Maureen Pisani Ph.D.
www.ProThriveSBH.com

177

I will have already discussed with the client what reaction/response they would like to have, so I'll have their own words to share with them. The closer to their own words the suggestions are, the easier it will be for their unconscious mind to accept and implement these suggestions.

I will repeat this technique with each of the scenarios or situations the clients used to struggle with. It is extremely important to reinforce the client feeling safe and calm in between each scenario.

I will also give reversals to re-lock the positive behaviors. Reversals will sound like: *"The more you try to behave in that old negative way, the faster you will accept these new beneficial ways of behaving, expressing yourself, and living. In fact, the more you try to stay the same, the faster these suggestions will be yours, permanently."*

Remember that the word "try" gives us permission to fail honorably. So, I only use the "T" word in reversals, because as soon as the clients' unconscious mind hears the word "try," they are going to fail at doing whatever follows the word, which in this case will make the reversals more powerful and effective.

Why it Works!
Maureen Pisani Ph.D.
www.ProThriveSBH.com

My intention, my plan, and my strategy when giving hypnotic suggestions is to make the acceptance of the new beneficial desired outcome beyond easy to accept, and that it makes the old negative behavior easier to release and/or be forgotten.

4. HOW TO OVERRIDE OLD TRIGGERS.

When we go through a traumatic experience, our mind locks in details about that experience of which we might not even be aware. These details are what the amygdala looks for as "danger signs/ red flags," because if any of those details show up in the client's life, the amygdala will go into high alert as a preventive mechanism, triggering the sympathetic nervous system into a survival mechanism. This is why people describe their P.T.S.D. incidents as haphazard and that they come on without warning, because it's all an unconscious programmed behavior intended to keep these individuals safe. Unfortunately, the resultant outcome is the exact opposite.

Not every detail that's exact to the original traumatic event will lead to another traumatic event, however. It might be that the trigger resembled a detail, and the response was launched.

Why it Works!
Maureen Pisani Ph.D.
www.ProThriveSBH.com

179

People's unconscious minds have only one intention – to keep us safe, so the re-triggering of all these potential red flags creates several intense responses to innocuous situations.

Let's say that a client witnessed a horrific shooting. Yes, it was traumatic and yes, it was appropriate for that client's amygdala to trigger their sympathetic nervous system that released all that adrenaline and cortisol so that that client could run like crazy and escape the intense danger. BUT... does that client's system need to go into a full-blown survival response if they are just hearing fireworks? The sound of the fireworks might be similar to the gun shots, but the client is in no immediate danger when watching fireworks from a distance and planning on just enjoying the display. Right?

Another example might be if the child's father had a very particular voice, and when he got upset and physically abused the children, he yelled, and his voice had a distinctive sound to it. It wouldn't be fair for the client to have that same reaction to being hit and yelled at by their abusive father, if someone in their world had a similar tone like their father, right?

Why it Works!
Maureen Pisani Ph.D.
www.ProThriveSBH.com

During the cognitive portion of the session, I make a list of the old experiences and what the client's triggers are nowadays. I get as many details as possible, as the more differentiators I have, the better the client's unconscious mind can separate the old from the new.

I work with the client to get statements that are factual and empowering. Sentences like, *"I am an adult now. I am in charge of me. I can and will always defend myself. I am free of my past. I am safe. I live in a safe neighborhood. I am safe in my home."*

Once in a hypnotic state, I walk the client through therapeutic guided visualizations where they initially observe themselves in a scenario. From this observational perspective, they ensure that the entire scenario is safe. Finally, they step into themselves and experience the event, while simultaneously confirming how safe they are, how safe they feel, and how safe and fully in control their body is. I repeat this process with each of the scenarios that in the past used to bother them and/or they reacted too intensely, and/or where they felt they lost control.

Once they go through the experience, then I walk them through how easy it is for them to react calmly, where

Why it Works!
Maureen Pisani Ph.D.
www.ProThriveSBH.com

181

their body (heartbeat, breathing and muscle tension) confirms that they are safe. I then have them visualize how they are reacting – with ease, happily, enjoying themselves, calmly observing, being in control, being empowered, being fully THEMSELVES and still being safe.

It is essential to get exactly how the client would like to respond, from the client. Never assume. What you might think of as appropriate might be completely outrageous for the client. When working cognitively with the client, if they cannot come up with adjectives to describe how they'd like to react to the situation, yes, you can offer words, but only use those words if the client agrees to them and approves them.

Remember that the unconscious mind hates unknowns and will fight tooth and nail against accepting unknowns, so no suggestions are given with a future tense. I never say, "at some point you will feel better," because it's too uncertain and that suggestion will only create more anxiety in the client's unconscious mind. I will take them out into an unspecified time in the future, where "a few days" could mean anything. After all a year is 365 days, which constitutes a few days, right?

Why it Works!
Maureen Pisani Ph.D.
www.ProThriveSBH.com

Once in the future, then my suggestions are in real time. *"You are seeing how a 4th of July barbeque celebration is fun and safe, right? Of course, you do! All your family, your loved ones, and friends are enjoying themselves, and see... so are you! You feel happy, you're enjoying the company, the jokes, the laughter, the good food. You're feeling fantastic, your body is calm and relaxed, your smile reaches your eyes, your heart is happy, and you REALLY LIKE this experience. And... look, now the fireworks are starting! Everyone's so excited about these fireworks, the displays are colorful and intricate. You hear the "oohs" and "aahs" from all the people around and you connect with, and experience, is happiness, togetherness, satisfaction of a day well spent, where hundreds of memories were made, and you received so much love and acceptance that you will always remember this day as a goooooooooood day!"*

This way not only have we nullified that the loud bangs are potentially dangerous, but that when the loud bangs are fireworks, the client has a new memory from which to draw positive associations and appropriate responses. I utilize this technique for as many triggers as the client has. Sometimes, the client's unconscious mind will generalize to similar events, so from the 4th of July

Why it Works!
Maureen Pisani Ph.D.
www.ProThriveSBH.com

183

barbeque it will extend this new behavior to family gatherings, or even parties with friends. However, if the triggers are vastly dissimilar – for example, family gatherings and doctors' appointments, then I will take the client through a similar script where doctors' offices, appointments, and treatments are all safe, and the client will have a new calm and peaceful response.

5. HOW TO INTRODUCE SELF-FORGIVENESS.

One of the things that keeps us stuck in our old behaviors is how we constantly judge ourselves negatively. We are our own judge, jury, and executioner. We find ourselves guilty and give ourselves the worst possible sentences. We never give ourselves the possibility of parole. We think of ourselves in the worst of ways and every time a situation arises where that memory is triggered, we once again run ourselves through the entire experience, once again giving ourselves the guilty verdict, reinforcing how bad we are.

As you can now appreciate this repetitive cycle demolishes all our Self-Identity. Each aspect –

Why it Works!
Maureen Pisani Ph.D.
www.ProThriveSBH.com

Confidence, Esteem, Acceptance, Respect, Worth and Love - is crushed by this relentless guilty verdict. But how is one supposed to break free? With realizations, understandings, appreciation, compassion, and love.

This is how I explain this situation to clients. Let's say that you have a negative memory that you judge yourself harshly on and this memory happened when you were 17 years of age.

I get the details of the situation. Usually, it is an incident that just happened, that wasn't intentional. I ask if at 17 years of age, that was the best decision that the client could make. Usually, the answer is yes, that's all they knew. The negative repercussions took them by surprise. They weren't prepared for them. The client hadn't even thought that those negative outcomes were possible, which is partly why they judge themselves so harshly today.

I ask the client to think back to when they were 17 years of age. Could they see how all they had were (for the sake of this exercise) 3 tools in the "toolbox of life," and that now at their current age, they have 12 tools in their toolbox of life, fair? They agree. So, I ask the client, would expecting the 17-year-old version of themselves

Why it Works!
Maureen Pisani Ph.D.
www.ProThriveSBH.com

185

to function in the same way they would now (knowing what information and capabilities [the 12 tools] they have now) be unfair to the teenage version of themselves? They agree. And... there it is. The understanding that when things happened in the past, they did what they thought was the best strategy at the time.

Our unconscious mind is constantly coming up with solutions, responses, and answers to whatever we are currently facing. However, it can only come up with these by utilizing the information we have at the time. A 17-year-old only has so much information, whereas a 35-year-old will have more.

However, a 70-year-old will have more insight than the 35-year-old, right?

There's a Maya Angelou quote, *"Do the best you can until you know better. Then when you know better, do better."* This sums up how I introduce compassion, understanding, and forgiveness to the clients. Holding onto to all that negative judgment not only keeps us stuck in the past but depletes our self-identity and limits how far we can rise.

Self-forgiveness is a liberating emotion. Allowing the forgiveness to wash over those memories releases the negative painful emotion.

Why it Works!
Maureen Pisani Ph.D.
www.ProThriveSBH.com

Forgiving ourselves allows for love to be accepted, opens us up to the realization that we have learned from then to now, which means that we can continue learning. We gift ourselves a future that is continually expanding, and one where we continue rising.

The more we learn, the more we understand, and the more we realize how much we don't know, which intensifies our curiosity to continue learning. The more information we accrue, as soon as we accept it and implement it, the sooner it is transformed into expertise and wisdom. As we incorporate all this wisdom into our everyday lives, we start seeing the silver linings in every cloud, we understand that our entire lives are a continuous learning experience, so mistakes are going to happen. We get to appreciate that mistakes are part of the learning process, so as long as we are doing better as we keep improving, we can forgive ourselves for our mistakes.

I get as much detail as I possibly can during the cognitive portion of the session. This could include what the client did, why they did it, what they expected, how it blew up in their face, all the fallout this incident created, how bad they felt, what they did in a desperate attempt to fix it, what worked, what didn't work, all those negative words they used to describe themselves, what others said, what others did, and how they still feel

Why it Works!
Maureen Pisani Ph.D.
www.ProThriveSBH.com

187

about it now. I usually ask a few questions, and the clients, as soon as they feel how relieving this unburdening is, will take the lead and just share. Taking notes is essential because during the hypnosis, it is imperative to use their own words. Replicating the client's vernacular will make the suggestions easier to be recognized, accepted, and implemented by their unconscious mind.

I do not share with the client what I am planning, because I don't want to give the unconscious mind an opportunity to panic and refuse to participate. However, I will share with you why I choose to utilize the Ho'oponopono technique for self-forgiveness.

The Ho'Oponopono technique is a Hawaiian family problem-solving tradition, used to restore harmony. The meaning of the word is Ho (to make) and pono (right). The double pono in the word is done to state that it is making things "doubly right." This is a process in which we can forgive others and ourselves.

The Ho'oponopono technique is to walk through four stages −

1- I'm sorry
2- Please forgive me
3- Thank you
4- I love you

Why it Works!
Maureen Pisani Ph.D.
www.ProThriveSBH.com

Yes, it is effective just as is, but I, believe that the more personalized the exercise, the more effective it will be, and the more forgiveness and resolution the client will have. So, I personalize this technique for each client.

Once in a hypnotic state, I have the client look in a mirror, so they are staring into their own eyes. I explain to them that they are the only ones who know the 100% truth, 100% of the wounds, the pain, the joys, and the love. I ask the client to take a moment and look at themselves with gratitude for having had the strength to make it through it all.

As they are appreciating themselves with gratitude, I say *".... now let these thoughts be as if they were your own,"* and I switch my language pattern to the "I" form. This way all subsequent suggestions are not only more intense, but are also received with less resistance, therefore making them easier to be accepted and implemented by the client's unconscious mind.

As I am walking them through each stage, in the first suggestion, I say their name, so it will sound like this: *"I'm sorry Jane. I'm truly sorry. I thought that staying quiet would make it all go away. I'm so sorry."* I plan to have at least 8-10 suggestions per segment. Once I've said all the suggestions for the "I'm sorry" segment, I will end it with *"I'm so sorry."*

Why it Works!
Maureen Pisani Ph.D.
www.ProThriveSBH.com

189

Yes, voice intonation is important. Someone who is truly sorry and contrite doesn't have a bubbly voice. Speak the suggestions with the intensity that shares how much you mean it. (I always put myself in the position that, if it were up to me to forgive this person, would I? Yes, I would. So, I speak every word with full meaning.)

Then I take the client through the next segment – "Please forgive me." The transition is seamless, as we go from one to the other where each new segment has the client's name stated. This intentional personalization brings it home for the client. Once I give the client all the suggestions for this segment, I lead them into the "Thank you" segment. Again, the first suggestion has their name added. We go through life being ignored, underappreciated, invalidated, and taken for granted, so hearing "thank you" repeatedly soothes the soul. After all the suggestions for the "thank you" segment have been completed, then I walk the client through the last segment - "I love you." This is probably the most impactful section of the exercise. I repeat the "I love you" phrase several times with each suggestion.

We live in a world where true love is rare, where the word "love" has been reduced to an adjective, where people toss the word around and hardly ever mean it.

Why it Works!
Maureen Pisani Ph.D.
www.ProThriveSBH.com

Clients have been betrayed and heartbroken because to them the word "love" carries a tremendous amount of weight and commitment, while to the other person, it was just a fancy word to use to get the client to acquiesce. As I walk them through the last portion of the exercise, where I reinforce how much they love themselves, most clients' response is that during that portion they start crying. True love is a rare experience, so when they are gifting true love to themselves, it transforms their lives.

As they continue listening to the hypnotic recording every evening, continuous forgiveness keeps occurring, which leads to higher levels of all Self-Identity attributes, which in turn leads to a better self-image. All this leads to a better day-to-day existence and an incredible future.

6. HOW TO BUILD ALL THE SELF-IDENTITY ATTRIBUTES.

Most people don't realize how low their Self-Identity is. They are going through life, doing their best, pushing themselves on a daily basis just to survive. When I introduce clients to the individual aspects of Self-Identity - Self-Confidence, Self-Esteem,

Why it Works!
Maureen Pisani Ph.D.
www.ProThriveSBH.com

191

Self-Acceptance, Self-Respect, Self-Worth, and Self-Love - most just look at me baffled. They might have heard of Self-Confidence or Self-Esteem, and sometimes ladies have heard of Self-Respect, but as for the other attributes, most people didn't even know they existed.

It's no wonder that if they didn't know that these attributes existed, it stands to reason that they couldn't have focused on them or made any effort to improve on them, right? This is where I explain what they are and how they affect each of our thoughts, decisions, and actions.

Usually, clients are eager to improve, so after listening to the introduction of a self-identity attribute, they ask me what they can do to improve the levels and/or live a better life which will, in turn, improve the levels.

I walk the clients through how loving themselves is never a bad thing. Initially, they agree, but we are both aware that the clients' day-to-day life is the opposite of self-love. The clients are usually selfless and give to others to the point of exhaustion. In this case, being that

Why it Works!
Maureen Pisani Ph.D.
www.ProThriveSBH.com

I know my clients, I will choose the lowest item on their priority list, which is usually their pet. I will ask if they could at least love themselves as much as they love their pet! That usually creates two responses – a chuckle, and then the realization hits - and they admit that even that much love would make a huge improvement in their life.

What I mean is that these people prioritize everyone and everything else ahead of themselves, because they love them and wish the best for them. BUT... if the client keeps giving, that person will at some point end up on "empty," and then if that individual is burnt out, who will be around to take care of all the others who the client loves so much? Usually, I get a head tilt to this comment, which means I've got their attention, they're listening, and they are curious to see where this is going... which also means that they are ready to hear an effective, efficient solution to this dilemma.

I use a very practical analogy here. I ask the clients what they do when their cell phone goes down to zero charge. They each easily and quickly respond, "Well, I charge it!" Correct answer. Then I ask the clients if their cell phone lost any of its value while it was being charged. They state that the phone doesn't lose any of its value while being charged. Again, correct answer. So, I take it home with the explanation that we get to benefit from the phone once it's fully charged.

Why it Works!
Maureen Pisani Ph.D.
www.ProThriveSBH.com

193

Taking care of oneself is exactly like charging one's phone. I ask if the clients are open to breaking down what they can do each day to ensure that their Self-Identity levels are restored and maintained at high levels. They agree.

Self-Identity is the combined result of how the following attributes function.

- SELF-CONFIDENCE.

This is based on how each of us answers the "Can I do it?" question. I share with the clients that all they have to do is look back into their past and see how much they accomplished. Most have a long list of things they've done, achieved, overcome, or gone through, so when they look back, they can honestly say "Knowing that I overcame that, I know I can do this."

This is a sure way to build Self-Confidence.

If the clients cannot give themselves credit for achieving anything, or are unsure of themselves, I will then walk them through the notion that they went through the four stages of learning in everything they do in their normal life.

Why it Works!
Maureen Pisani Ph.D.
www.ProThriveSBH.com

They began by being unconsciously incompetent, where they didn't know what they didn't know. (A 2-year-old has no clue what it takes to drive a car.) Then, after their first driver's education session, they hit the second stage of learning, where they became consciously incompetent. They realized how much they didn't know. After a few more lessons, they advanced to the third stage of being consciously competent. They knew what to do, but it was still mechanical. They had to think about it to do it. Finally, after a few months, they achieved the fourth and final stage of learning, where they became unconsciously competent. Driving to these clients had become second nature.

I explain to the clients that knowing that they went through all four stages and achieved full competence with driving, brushing their teeth, tying their shoelaces, and many more activities they do daily and without thinking, they can definitely learn to do "____," or whatever they set their mind to.

This realization builds their Self-Confidence tremendously.

I also ask if there ever was something that was daunting to them at the time that they were learning it, and it was

Why it Works!
Maureen Pisani Ph.D.
www.ProThriveSBH.com

195

a tremendous achievement for them to have completed it and passed with flying colors. If they have a memory of that kind, that's the example I will utilize in the hypnotic suggestions. If they did *that*, then they can definitely do this.

- SELF-ESTEEM.

This is when we answer the "Do I deserve the best?" question. Self-Esteem is based on what people think they deserve. When faced with a dilemma, people will internally ask if they deserve the mediocre, the average, the improved, or the best. Most will choose one of the first three choices, and only the individuals with high levels of Self-Esteem will choose the last choice – the best.

It all stems from how individuals perceived the life they were living…not how life really was, but how they perceived it. Children, who are going through life with a brain that is still growing, face countless situations that are new, unknown, and open to interpretation. I ask the clients why they don't believe they deserve the best. Most have a memory etched in their mind, where something happened and the conclusion, they came up with was that what they received was exactly what they deserved.

Why it Works!
Maureen Pisani Ph.D.
www.ProThriveSBH.com

It's completely irrelevant whether that was the correct conclusion they could come to, because it was the conclusion they did come to, and it tipped the basis for how they experienced everything else that followed that incident.

So, I gently ask them, *"What could you have possibly done in your past to deserve such deplorable treatment? Have you murdered anyone? Have you intentionally stolen from people? Or cheated others just to hurt them?"* As soon as I start asking questions, the clients usually are sitting on the edge of their seats shouting, *"Oh no!"* very strongly! That's exactly the response I was looking for.

Then I continue with, *"So, If you haven't done anything so awful, why don't you think you deserve the best?"* At this point, the clients are quiet. Some become pensive, others have tears streaming down their faces, while others just look at me with that quizzical look of having deep understandings starting to register in their mind.

Once in hypnosis, I give suggestions to enhance all self-identity attributes, but especially, Self-Esteem. I share how now, they themselves have acknowledged how deserving they are, and because they decided that it was acceptable, it's theirs. From this point on, they will live life from the perspective that they are truly deserving …of the best, always.

Why it Works!
Maureen Pisani Ph.D.
www.ProThriveSBH.com

197

- SELF- ACCEPTANCE.

This attribute helps us recognize who we truly are, what our strengths and weaknesses are, and how we function through life. If our self-acceptance is low, then we are unaccepting of who we are. This could be one of two scenarios: (i) either we are refusing to acknowledge the positive aspect of who we are, or (ii) we are aware of the positive but ignore it completely, only to judge ourselves relentlessly because of our weaknesses and negative aspects. Either way, this is an incredibly unfair perspective to live by. I have had clients who despised themselves so much that they voiced that in their opinion, they shouldn't be alive. Yes, this is very serious.

I ask the client what their weaknesses are, and they can rattle them off to me in a few brief sentences. Then I ask them what their strengths are, and clients usually have a lot of difficulty connecting with them. This is when I start suggesting positive qualities that I know the clients own, so as I ask if "__" is a strength they have, they can easily say "yes." I keep going, asking, suggesting, and getting acceptance and approval for several traits. I will make sure that the list of strengths is longer than the list of weaknesses. They are working with me to improve their self-acceptance, so I am going to make sure that they realize how much good they have in themselves.

Why it Works!
Maureen Pisani Ph.D.
www.ProThriveSBH.com

After I suggest a few strengths, usually the clients then start adding more strengths and attributes themselves. All I say then is, *"and what other strengths do you have?"* and they continue adding more. After a while, when the list of strengths is sufficiently long and the clients are starting to loop (bringing up the same traits again), I change my question to, *"Are there any other strengths you'd like to add?"* and after a couple of moments I'll just ask, *"Anything else? Is there anything else you'd like to add?"* By this point, I've made sure that they have brought up all the attributes that were relevant to them.

In hypnosis, I will reiterate the strengths list, finishing it off with *"...and as you remember more, you'll keep adding them to this list."* This way, their mind will remain open to learning, acknowledging, and accepting more positive traits about themselves.

Having high levels of self-acceptance does not mean becoming grandiose in self-imagery. Quite the contrary, in fact. High levels of self-acceptance present in a way where one knows what one's capabilities are and what other things one cannot do. So it could be that Jane accepts that she's a phenomenal calculus instructor but won't attempt to fix a plumbing problem in her home,

Why it Works!
Maureen Pisani Ph.D.
www.ProThriveSBH.com

199

because she's aware that she has no clue about plumbing. It could be that Peter is aware of how amazing he is with cars and their engines but knows that he's out of his depth when it comes to doing his own tax returns.

Being aware of where the line in the sand is makes for a smoother lifestyle, where individuals take on the topics in which they are proficient, and delegate the topics in which they are aware they are inexperienced.

Having high levels of self-acceptance improves the quality of life, improves our sense of humor, makes us more relatable to others, and helps us love ourselves more.

- SELF-RESPECT.

This is when how we think of ourselves creates our thinking, our decisions, and our actions. We learn about respect from observing how others talk about it. When a person is being disrespectful, we hear about the incident. When young people misbehave, especially in sexual situations, we have all heard the comment, "they wouldn't have done that if they at least respected themselves!"

Why it Works!
Maureen Pisani Ph.D.
www.ProThriveSBH.com

However, growing up, hardly anyone is taught how to respect themselves. Yes, I would assume that the British Royal Family instills self-respect in their children, but as a norm, most parents raise their children with what's right and what's wrong; what's acceptable and what isn't. Hardly are the words *"This is how you need to behave to strengthen how much you respect yourself!"* We have, however, heard, *"That behavior is disrespectful to you, to me, and to your entire family!"*

Self-Respect is somewhat of a hidden trait that is strengthened or weakened by our behaviors. However, the initial levels of self-respect are set by how others treat us. Acknowledging that we don't know what is right or wrong as babies, we just accept what is. If there are abusive parents in the household, that child might erroneously conclude that abusive behavior is appropriate. So, when they grow up and they are in an abusive relationship, it's not that they don't have any self-respect. That's what their unconscious mind deemed appropriate because that's what it was used to receiving in the past.

Why it Works!
Maureen Pisani Ph.D.
www.ProThriveSBH.com

201

If, however, a family raises a child with standards of what is and isn't acceptable, what language is or isn't appropriate, when that child is in different scenarios and foul language is used, that child's self-respect will kick in and they will be able to differentiate who is respecting them and who is insulting them.

There are other times where self-respect is essential as a boundary against abusers who also carry high-intensity titles – Mom, Dad, Sister, Brother, Husband, Wife, Son, or Daughter, to mention the main ones. When a person owning one of these titles abuses a loved one, that person finds themselves in conflict. The person being attacked on one hand, appreciates that being abused is wrong, but then that person's heart strings are pulled because the abuser is also "___," supposedly a person from the inner circle of life, where people are supposed to be safe people, who love that person, not abuse them.

There's a sentence that I heard a while back that brings all this into focus: *"The quality of life we live depends on the behavior we accept."* At some point there needs to be a realization of how unacceptable the abuse is, and

Why it Works!
Maureen Pisani Ph.D.
www.ProThriveSBH.com

that the person being attacked needs to take a stand. I appreciate that this is a difficult decision to make, but here's what I will ask you, the reader. If that person's mother was abusing them, doesn't that mother also have the responsibility to honor the mother-child relationship? And if the person being attacked took a stand to honor their self-respect and stand their ground, how is that a negative action?

Here's how I explain it to clients.

Standing up for oneself in these situations is about protecting oneself by removing themselves from abusive situations. Instead of retaliating and striking back, removing oneself from abusive surroundings is a sure way to ensure one's safety. The abusers usually will still blame the target of their abuse, to come out as the victims not the attackers. Only the ones being attacked know the full story and the full extent of how abusive the situation really was. The abusers never admit to the full intensity of their abuse. At the risk of sounding repetitive, removing oneself without retaliating is the best course of action for most. Plus, people who abuse and claim to love the person they are abusing are completely oblivious to the oxymoron they're stating. Abuse and love are incompatible with each other.

Why it Works!
Maureen Pisani Ph.D.
www.ProThriveSBH.com

203

Removing oneself, cutting cords, and declining to participate in family functions, are all acts of honoring one's self-respect.

Nowhere have I stated to attack the abuser back, to lash out at them, slander them, or to go to family functions and create a scene. Refraining from retaliation is also part of self-respect. The person being attacked will emerge triumphant and honorable at the end of the day because each of us ultimately, will be judged according to what OUR actions were, not what others did to us. Keeping that in mind allows the person being abused to walk with their head held high, knowing that their hands and their conscience are clean.

Why it Works!
Maureen Pisani Ph.D.
www.ProThriveSBH.com

- SELF-WORTH.

This is where how we think of ourselves determines the quality of life we live. Self-worth is the resultant effect of what we observed and experienced during our childhood and adolescence. It translates into what we deem is acceptable for us, from what living situation we choose, what clothing we wear, what vehicle we drive, all the way to what we eat daily.

As we're growing up, we're observing. We are aware of what home looks like, how clean/messy it is, what the standards that are kept in the house are, what is found acceptable and what isn't. However, we also see how other homes are kept, what the condition of the home and its contents are, and how the people who live there talk about their belongings. There are people who will accept everything and anything, as long as it makes do. These people will have all kinds of furniture that aren't used for their purpose. They might have a bedroom bureau functioning as a TV stand, because for them that's what they were looking for, and ultimately, they're happy because the "that'll do" attitude solved their problem. There are other people, however, who will search high and low to obtain the exact piece of furniture that is the right color and has the correct design. Then and only then will they accept that it's the right piece for them and buy it.

Why it Works!
Maureen Pisani Ph.D.
www.ProThriveSBH.com

205

This is an incredibly superficial way to explain self-worth, because this trait affects our decisions across the board in more important aspects of our lives.

High levels of self-worth are what makes a person leave their romantic partner as soon as they find out that their partner cheated on them. Low levels will have that person rationalizing that the cheater had their reasons, maybe even blame themselves, and end up tolerating all kinds of abuse, literally risking their lives health-wise just to be able to stay in the relationship. The people with low levels of self-worth tolerate most everything in a relationship because they believe that's all they deserve.

Self-worth also affects what we tolerate, accept, or refute in all relationships, not just romantic ones, but relationships with family, in business, and professional relationships. Think of what happened with all the scandals in Hollywood that led to the "MeToo" movement. There were thousands of women over decades who had been abused, molested, raped, intimidated, and blacklisted when they wouldn't comply with sexual advances or submit to the abuse. During those times, it was unthinkable for a woman to stand up and say "NO!"

Why it Works!
Maureen Pisani Ph.D.
www.ProThriveSBH.com

The norm was to submit, stay silent, and at best, walk away. However, one day, one lady did say "NO!" publicly, one lady who had high levels of self-worth, and thanks to her, more stood up, more said "NO!" and that abusive, perverted system was broken.

These scenarios happen across the planet in every aspect of life. There will always be people who think they can get away with whatever they desire. Yes, there will be men and women who abuse others. Yes, there will be some who will submit and stay silent, but there is always ONE whose levels of self-worth are strong, who says, "Enough is enough" and speaks up. As soon as that one person speaks up, others show up.

It doesn't have to a massive movement, or such a drastic topic…living with high levels of self-worth can transform one's life even in the little things. One can determine with whom they spend time. They can surround themselves with people who are negative and unmotivated, who bring their energy down, or with people who are positive, optimistic, and driven, that makes one's life better.

Here's how I like to explain life to my clients. You know the saying, "People come into your life for a reason, a season, or a lifetime." If you can imagine that each of us is walking on a pathway that is our life, you can see how some people show up in our lives, and that's when their pathway and ours merge.

Why it Works!
Maureen Pisani Ph.D.
www.ProThriveSBH.com

207

However, when that person's season is over and they leave, you can see how their pathway would split away from ours. Fair? Our lives are pathways that are constantly merging with and splitting away from other pathways. Having high levels of self-worth puts people in a position to recognize that if the person we're walking through life with is treating us poorly, then it's more than acceptable for us to walk away. When pathways split away, it's more than ok.

I'm not saying to stop talking to everyone you know, on the contrary, cherish the people who respect you, who honor you, who celebrate you! You're worthy of that!

- **SELF-LOVE.**

This is where how much we love ourselves translates into the reality we live. This trait is probably the most misunderstood self-identity attribute.

For a long time, people have been living their lives juggling so many things, being everything to so many people, that their lives end up being a constant race against the clock where the to-do list is never completely done.

Most of these people are living this lifestyle because they love the people in their lives. However, it does backfire on them.

Why it Works!
Maureen Pisani Ph.D.
www.ProThriveSBH.com

At some point, these individuals run out of fuel, hit empty, and burnout happens (because it always does), and the people that these individuals were doing everything for are left high and dry, which is basically what these individuals were working so hard to prevent.

These individuals love everyone but have low levels of self-love. They put themselves last on the list, and because there were so many other important priorities that simply had to be dealt with, they never got around to taking care of themselves.

Self-love is often seen as pampering or being conceited, where running oneself ragged is seen as selfless. This occurs the most with loving, devoted Moms. These ladies do their utmost to take care of the kids, their partner, and the house, while also juggling their job and/or career. There isn't enough time in a day to manage everything and also include having some down time for mom. These women usually respond with *"Well, isn't sleeping my downtime?"* Yes, it is definitely downtime, but usually, these women are beyond exhausted by the time it's time for sleep, so sleeping in this case isn't an act of self-love, but more of a survival requirement.

Why it Works!
Maureen Pisani Ph.D.
www.ProThriveSBH.com

209

Instilling and maintaining high levels of self-love is essential for everyone involved. The people who invest in taking care of themselves with intention, who implement those acts of self-love, will have more energy and therefore more resilience. They will be more positive, they will feel better, and will therefore be healthier and will enjoy life so their own, and their family's quality of life will improve.

What actions am I referring to, you ask? Self-love doesn't have to be a drawn-out expensive experience, although I would recommend that if that person can afford it. Spending a few days at an exclusive resort tends to fill up all reservoirs where self-love will be replenished.

However, there are countless things people can do to replenish and strengthen their self-love. These could include but are not limited to – scheduling and getting regular manicures & pedicures, massages, blocking time daily to enjoy their favorite tea in peace and quiet, going to the gym, attending their favorite yoga class, carving out time daily to read or listen to an audiobook, taking the time to prepare their favorite smoothie, prioritizing an activity for themselves, watching their favorite movie/show, making that extra effort to ensure

Why it Works!
Maureen Pisani Ph.D.
www.ProThriveSBH.com

their health (this could be exercising, taking a break or even meditating), spending time with their loved ones, allocating time for their hobbies, and many more. I suggest to my clients to ask themselves what makes their heart happy, and that's what they need to do.

When selfless people come to me, I listen to how much they do for all the people that they love. Then I ask them if they know of any marathon runners who sprint the entire 26.2 miles of the race. They look at me quizzically and cautiously respond with, *"No. Marathon runners never sprint. They have to pace themselves if they plan on finishing the race."* That's the correct answer. All I do is smile and gently highlight how they are running a lifelong marathon which is longer than 26.2 miles. Pacing themselves IS self-love.

I ask them which outcome they wish to have...would they rather go nonstop 24/7 and then crash and crumble, leaving their loved ones high and dry? Or would they rather pace themselves, where they continue to thrive and be healthy enough to continue caring for their loved ones for the rest of their lives? That's when the smiles show up and I know they got it. That's when I recommend making a list of things/activities they are going to introduce and maintain in their daily lives that will enhance their quality of life, improve their health, and strengthen their resilience.

Why it Works!
Maureen Pisani Ph.D.
www.ProThriveSBH.com

211

Self-Love truly is an attribute we all need to have in our lives.

7. HOW TO ENSURE THAT NEW BEHAVIORS ARE INSTALLED & IMPLEMENTED.

When clients come in for Hypnotherapy, they are usually at a point in life where they are aware that something's not working for them, that they have a habit or a pattern that's detrimental to them and they'd like to get rid of it, and/or they would like to improve an aspect of their life – either personally or professionally, or both.

Either way, they all have the status quo, and they all have their desired future life that they'd like to create. There are things hypnotherapists need to keep in mind to ensure that these new behaviors are installed and implemented in their clients' unconscious minds.

Here are my techniques on how I guide my clients' conscious and unconscious minds, both during the cognitive and hypnotic portions of the session.

Why it Works!
Maureen Pisani Ph.D.
www.ProThriveSBH.com

SAFE.

As you are now aware, survival mechanisms are triggered as soon as we feel threatened. As soon as the 5F's are launched, we drop down to being reactive instead of proactive. I have also explained that the unconscious mind is terrified of unknown experiences. Its response to instilling new behaviors, new responses, and even new ways of thinking, albeit positive and empowering, is to reject what it doesn't know and ultimately doesn't trust to be safe.

That's exactly the secret combination to making these new behaviors acceptable. They have to be seen, assessed, and confirmed to be safe to the person's unconscious mind. Then and only then will they be accepted, owned, and implemented in the clients' everyday lives.

As their hypnotherapist, I always ask the clients what they would like to add or remove from their lives and why, can they visualize how their life will be after they implement that decision, and is it safe for them? As they are describing their desired future, I take notes because using their own wording is also part of how fast their unconscious mind will accept and implement these scenarios into their lives.

Why it Works!
Maureen Pisani Ph.D.
www.ProThriveSBH.com

213

I remember having a client who came to me for weight reduction. During the first session, as I was getting to know her and understand her goals, I asked, *"Oh, so… would you like to be skinny, or having tighter, smoother contours?"* The client jolted upright in her chair and responded forcefully with *"Never skinny! Those cheerleaders at high school were skinny and they were bitches!"* If I hadn't asked and had used the word "skinny" in my hypnotic suggestions, because of the client's association with the word, everything I would have said would have been rejected. However, because I took the time to confirm and delineate exactly what the client desired, I was able to utilize appropriate and acceptable wording for her mind to deem safe and therefore implementable. This resulted in the client reducing her weight and achieving her goal.

SECONDARY GAIN.

During the cognitive portion of the session, when the client and I are planning and strategizing their improved future, I ask them to imagine that I'm a fairy and that with my magic wand I went "Poof!" and their wishes were granted right now. Then I ask, how would their life be? This is an incredibly important question to ask, because their response highlights if they have any secondary gain.

Why it Works!
Maureen Pisani Ph.D.
www.ProThriveSBH.com

If the client responds with, *"Oh! That would be fantastic! I'll be living my best life! Bring it on! I'll be so happy!"* That response shows me that there is no secondary gain, where the client is truly ready to move onwards and upwards. Their answer, incidentally, will make it easier for their unconscious mind to accept and implement the hypnotic suggestions.

If, however, the client responds with, *"Well... that's tough. I've been in this situation for so long, I can't even begin to imagine how my life would look like or how I'd feel without this "___" that I'm dealing with."* That response highlights that the client is receiving something that their unconscious mind values and sees as a benefit. Here's an example. A woman who is capable and strong and has managed her family and career all her life successfully, ends up having her family see her as completely self-sufficient and so they never offer to help. Then, one day the woman is diagnosed with an illness, and the family takes care of her, does all the housework, and spends time with her. That woman is receiving the attention she so desperately desired but never received. All that attention, even though it occurred because she's sick, is what her unconscious mind values and receives as secondary gain. Because of that benefit, that woman won't get better, because in her unconscious mind, getting better means returning to that place where her family ignored her, neglected her, and took her for granted.

Why it Works!
Maureen Pisani Ph.D.
www.ProThriveSBH.com

215

Please keep in mind that all this is unconscious and never intentional. As their hypnotherapist, it is incumbent upon me to walk the clients gently through how they *can* release the problem and still receive that valuable treatment. I never share with the client that they do have secondary gain, because being that they are processing all this unconsciously, saying those two words is received as a negative judgment. I present it in a way where I highlight the benefit – in the example above, it was how the family rallied around her, and how much help and attention she received, right? So, I ask the clients, what can they say or do to ensure that such attention and help continues? As soon as the clients come up with a solution where they can continue receiving the benefits after they overcome the presenting complaint we're working on... their unconscious mind is open to releasing the "__" (illness, habit, pattern).

ASSESSMENT WORDING.

During the cognitive portion of the session as the clients and I are working on why they desire this upgrade, and/or why do they think that now is the right time, and are they ready, I also ask them these questions:

Why it Works!
Maureen Pisani Ph.D.
www.ProThriveSBH.com

(i)   What will you gain if you stay the same?
(ii) What will you lose if you stay the same?
(iii) What will you gain when you implement this upgrade?
(iv) What will you lose when you implement this upgrade?

These questions are very intentionally worded. Yes, I am getting the clients' conscious minds to ponder different aspects of where they are. Everything in life has advantages and disadvantages. We are usually aware of the advantages but tend to turn a blind eye to the disadvantages because we are intentionally choosing that behavior. So, when I ask, "what will you gain and/or lose," I'm getting their minds to look at both aspects of the situation. I also ask IF they stay the same. IF is very weak, so even as I'm asking them, and yes this is still during the cognitive portion of the session, their conscious mind is already processing that this behavior is about to be released.

Then I ask, "WHEN you IMPLEMENT this UPGRADE". Each word is chosen with intention. "When" is implying that there's a time set for it to happen. "Implement" is the action word that the clients' unconscious mind needs to know what to do with all this.

Why it Works!
Maureen Pisani Ph.D.
www.ProThriveSBH.com

217

"Upgrade" is preferred and more acceptable than "change." "Upgrade" implies that the new way is going to beneficial for that individual. "Change" simply means different, which could be either good or bad, safe or dangerous, and that's why people's unconscious minds reject change. That's why people react negatively to "change" but wait in line for "upgrades."

Once the clients and I have discussed all four questions, and they have thought about what they will gain as soon as it's all implemented into their lives, those upgrades override any of the possible losses they had come up with earlier. Then, visualizing their new future is well within their safety parameters and therefore is acceptable to their unconscious mind.

FULL SENSORY EXPERIENCE.

Once the client is in a hypnotic state, I get them to create an image of their BEST SELF. I help guide them into creating while being simultaneously vague. Here's what I say: *"I would now like you to visualize your best future, where you at your best health, best love, best success, best wealth, best life, best...of...everything! Make it big, make it bright, make it 3D!"* This way if their unconscious mind is going "what best," I guide them through which aspects of life should be included in their visualization.

Why it Works!
Maureen Pisani Ph.D.
www.ProThriveSBH.com

However, never do I say how much wealth, what their best health is, or who their best love is. I keep all that vague so as not to limit them in any way. This way, each time they re-listen to the recording, they can adjust the details, or even incorporate new aspects into it. This makes the recording as personalized and adaptable as possible.

As soon as they have created the visualization, I walk them through experiencing it with all their senses. The more they experience their best future and the safer they feel while experiencing their best future, the easier it is for their unconscious mind to accept all the suggestions and implement it into their reality.

Each of us has five senses, but not all of us are primarily visual. If I had to only say "look at your best future," but the client happens to be primarily auditory or kinesthetic, my suggestion will not have the desired impact. That's why once they have created the visualization of their best future, I say, *"Now.... Taste it, smell it, feel it, hear it and see it!"* This way I ensure that all five senses are involved.

Why it Works!
Maureen Pisani Ph.D.
www.ProThriveSBH.com

219

I give the client about 15-20 seconds to create the visualization and an additional 15-20 seconds to experience it, after which I say, *"Now, as you experience it, notice how safe it is for you. So, as you continue going through it, allow these thoughts to be as if they were your own. 'I **like** this! I **accept** this! I **AM** this!'"*

The client created their best future, they experienced it, they acknowledged that it is safe for them to live, and with the last three sentences they're giving full permission for their unconscious mind to accept and implement all the suggestions.

Remember that the unconscious mind is terrified of unknowns, so its first response to unknown experiences is to reject them at all costs. Even if that unknown is a huge promotion with a huge financial raise, the unconscious mind cannot conceive how safe that amount of money is, because that individual never earned that kind of money before. The solution to that is to have the client initially work through all the cognitive work, but then to have the client go through this visualization exercise to experience it fully and deem it safe. Then and only then will the client's unconscious mind be open to receiving that financial abundance into their reality.

Why it Works!
Maureen Pisani Ph.D.
www.ProThriveSBH.com

COME FROM THE FUTURE.

As I've already explained, the unconscious mind dislikes and refuses to accept unknown experiences. When working with clients, we are always looking to improve their future but projecting into the future instantly triggers the unconscious homeostasis mechanism which blocks any forward movement into the unknown.

To overcome this hurdle, I have practiced taking the client into the future, where the client is already living the end result, and then I walk them backwards, reverse engineering the entire journey. Each step backward will describe the action taken, but I'm always coming from the perspective that every step of the way was safe, beneficial, successful, and already implemented. As I take the client through this reverse journey, each "new" action that I'm presenting to the unconscious is being described as a tried-and-true technique that led to the ultimate of success.

Here's how I present it: *"I'd like you to see yourself in this spacious corner office. You're sitting in a large executive chair, you're relaxing, and your feet are on the corner of your impressive desk.*

Why it Works!
Maureen Pisani Ph.D.
www.ProThriveSBH.com

221

You realize that you're smiling...you think back to that younger version of you. Remember how you dreamed of having this kind of lifestyle? Of course, you do! It's like it was yesterday! Yet... how exactly did you get here?

Oh, that's right... your professional track record is impressive, your reputation is impeccable. But how did that happen? Oh yes... you rose through your first company faster than anyone in its history! But how were you able to pull that off? Oh... because of your impressive work ethic and your dedication to always going the extra mile. But...how did you get that position? Oh yes... because you graduated with flying colors and your reputation preceded you!" This way the "unknowns" are being introduced to the unconscious mind as pragmatic and effective and definitely safe to implement.

When I bring the client all the way to where they are currently, I continue with, *"Now, take a moment and remember that younger version of you...the one who had the dreams, the drive, the stamina, the "unstoppability." Think of that version of you and thank them, because you know that it's thanks to that version of you and their perseverance that you are living this incredibly amazing life. Take a few moments and thank them from your heart."*

Why it Works!
Maureen Pisani Ph.D.
www.ProThriveSBH.com

Remember that suggestions given in a hypnotic state are in the client's unconscious mind. We also know that the unconscious mind does not differentiate fact from fiction. The only time it puts the brakes on is when it feels unsafe. Utilizing this technique removes all fears and all uncertainties while reinforcing that yes, the client will succeed, so each step delineated (in the reverse order) is safe to implement.

ANCHORS.

We have all faced the daunting "learning curve," where even though it is our own decision to learn something new, going through the learning stages is so incredibly annoying and tiresome that some of us stop practicing the new thing, and before you know it's history. We set New Year's Resolutions with the full intention to implement this new behavior into our daily life, but by mid-February, 80% of those resolutions have been discarded, forgotten, and/or have been labeled as failed resolutions. So how are we supposed to implement these upgrades and maintain them?

Hypnotherapy has a way of locking in behaviors that makes it easier for clients to achieve and maintain their goals. Hypnotherapy has "anchors," which are when movements, behaviors, or actions are linked to triggering their new behavior.

Why it Works!
Maureen Pisani Ph.D.
www.ProThriveSBH.com

223

There are some practitioners who create individualized poses or movements, like touching their thumb to a specific finger, or tugging on an earlobe. However, I prefer to anchor the new behavior to a process that the client does automatically, daily, if not several times during the day.

During the cognitive portion of the session, I observe the client and note what movements (fixing their hair, adjusting their glasses, playing with their rings, biting their lips, playing with their phone/pen, crossing right over left leg, licking their lips, etc.) are natural to the client. Yes, I'm looking for things that the client does naturally.

Once in a hypnotic state, then I anchor those actions into the new behavior. I also add what I know are normal activities, habits, and patterns we have nowadays. This is an example of what I say: *"Each and every time you fix your hair, adjust your glasses, pick up your phone, pick up your keys, open your car door, close your car door, turn on the ignition, click your seatbelt, walk in and out of a doorway, sit or stand, you will quadruple your motivation, determination, and implementation."* This way I'm closing the loophole so that if the client forgets the unique movement, they (i) don't think that all that effort put into the session is lost and (ii) don't think that they're failures.

Why it Works!
Maureen Pisani Ph.D.
www.ProThriveSBH.com

Because I've anchored normal, everyday actions, my suggestions will be re-triggered and reinforced each and every time they do these actions. This will lead to the clients implementing the new behavior easily and effortlessly.

REVERSALS.

One of the Laws of Hypnotherapy is the Law of Reverse Action. I love utilizing this law because it closes all loopholes and reinforces forward movement and success. As I get to know the client, I find out what their weaknesses are and what they fear will be their downfall. (For example, if a client is working on weight reduction and has been consistent with his/her results, but is terrified of falling off the wagon on Thanksgiving Day, that's precisely what I'm going to use in my reversal.)

Here's what I say: *"The harder you try to overeat during Thanksgiving dinner, the more steadfast to your healthy eating pattern you will stay, and the more aware of portion size you will be."*

If a client is fighting anxiety and depression, here's what I give as a suggestion: *"The harder you try to drop down into the negative emotions, the more here in neutral you will stay, and the more curious you will be to experience the positive emotions."*

Why it Works!
Maureen Pisani Ph.D.
www.ProThriveSBH.com

225

Reversals are extremely handy to solidify the desired behavior, while nullifying the weak behavior. As soon as I use the word "try," anything that follows it will be deemed to fail.

It is truly an incredible law to implement in each session. Utilizing reversals is a sure way to give the client's unconscious mind the support and guidance it needs to know what to do when the client is facing the temptation of choosing whether to stand fast and move forward into success or give in and slide down the slippery slope to the same old, same old. Reverting to what the client has been used to is the ultimate of failures.

I WONDER.

Even though most of us are polite and usually acquiesce to other's opinions or desires, each of us comes to the point where we are going to do whatever it is we want to do. Most of us become incredibly rebellious when we are told what to do, and regardless of whether the advice is sound or poor, and simply because we were told to do it, we refuse to do it. The way out of this instinctive rebellion and refusal of accepting suggestions is to offer the client's unconscious mind a choice.

Why it Works!
Maureen Pisani Ph.D.
www.ProThriveSBH.com

After I've given all the suggestions to the client and before I go into the sleep suggestions (better sleep is good for everyone, always), I allow a couple of seconds of silence, which apart from being an automatic deepener, also allows for the mind to become even more curious, which makes it even more eager to accept suggestions. Here's what I say: *"So, as you're relaxing, listening to my voice, I wonder ... are you going to accept all of these suggestions right now, or at 8:08 AM tomorrow morning? Or will you accept them at 11:11 AM tomorrow or will it be 5:55 PM? I'll let your unconscious mind decide."* This way it sounds like I've given the client's unconscious mind a choice, but I've also locked in that their unconscious mind WILL accept the suggestions, but at a time of their choice. This pseudo-choice gives the client's unconscious mind the impression that it is their decision, which enhances acceptance, but it is also limited to a specific timeframe, which removes all possibility of procrastination.

When it comes to which times I use, I have several. Each has a metaphysical significance. When I use 8:08 – it's implying permanence because the number 8 sideways becomes the infinity symbol. However, I cannot use 8:88 because that time doesn't exist.

Why it Works!
Maureen Pisani Ph.D.
www.ProThriveSBH.com

227

When I use 5:55 AM/PM, I'm strengthening the numerological value of 5 – "Chaos to Creation." I use this time when the client is going through a breakthrough. When I use 11:11AM/PM or 2:22 AM/PM or 3:33 AM/PM, I'm bringing in angelic numbers, which will then reinforce the blessings for the clients and their outcomes.

SPEAK IN THE "I" FORM.

Each of us, at the moment of truth, has heard that voice in our head saying, "You can do it!" or "What!?!? You think you can do that??" That voice is with us 24/7, 365. Ironically, it's the voice we listen to the most. I have found that when I give suggestions in the "" form, the client's unconscious mind tends to accept suggestions even faster than before.

As children we must listen and obey the adults, whether they are our parents, adult relatives, or teachers. However, as adults ourselves, we tend to filter what everyone tells us because on some level we believe that we really do know what's best for ourselves.

I have found that giving suggestions to the client in a toned-down whispering voice and in the "I" form

Why it Works!
Maureen Pisani Ph.D.
www.ProThriveSBH.com

transforms my suggestions into what the client's unconscious mind perceives as the client's own thoughts! This makes the hypnotic suggestions easier to accept and implement into the client's life.

Why it Works!
Maureen Pisani Ph.D.
www.ProThriveSBH.com

229

CHAPTER 8

STATISTICS & STATISTICAL ANALYSIS

One of the requirements of any research is the gathering of statistics and the sharing of the statistical analysis from the data gathered. I sent out a survey to my clients asking them to respond truthfully to the questions. As their hypnotherapist I guaranteed their anonymity – when they are working with me, afterwards, and in this case, when they responded to the survey.

The following are the results.

QUESTION	PERCENTAGE
How much did you know about Hypnotherapy before going for your first session with me?	
Nothing at all	12.89%
Had heart about it	59.84%
Had sessions before	27.27%

Why it Works!
Maureen Pisani Ph.D.
www.ProThriveSBH.com

QUESTION	PERCENTAGE
What aspect of life did you focus on when receiving Hypnotherapy?	
Health	33.33%
Relationships	25.00%
Stress	23.90%
Money	5.55%
Success	12.22%

Which of the following words would you use to describe the results of your hypnotherapy session?	
Satisfactory	14.29%
Great	26.53%
Surprising	25.85%
Outstanding	33.33%

Why it Works!
Maureen Pisani Ph.D.
www.ProThriveSBH.com

231

QUESTION	PERCENTAGE
How quickly did you start seeing results?	
About what I expected	44.03%
Faster than expected	29.85%
Surprisingly fast	26.12%

Overall, how satisfied are you with the results you experienced after receiving Hypnotherapy?	
20%	6.81%
40%	5.30%
60%	10.61%
80%	26.52%
100%	50.76%

Why it Works!
Maureen Pisani Ph.D.
www.ProThriveSBH.com

QUESTION	PERCENTAGE
How long did you continue listening to your personalized recording?	
Not at all	9.02%
A few days	12.78%
A few weeks	23.31%
A few months	30.83%
Still listening to it	24.06%
How long did the results last?	
1-11 months	38.64%
1-5 years	15.15%
6-10 years	0.80%
11-15 years	0.00%
Still going	45.41%

Why it Works!
Maureen Pisani Ph.D.
www.ProThriveSBH.com

233

QUESTION	PERCENTAGE
How likely is it that you would recommend Hypnotherapy to a friend, family member or colleague?	
25%	6.82%
55%	12.88%
85%	80.30%
Percentage of total responses has a margin of error of 0.1-0.4%	

As one can see, the results speak for themselves. Hypnotherapy produces consistent results in all areas of life. Listening to the hypnotic recording regularly enhances the maintenance of the results. Even when the clients had only heard about it, they were curious enough to give Hypnotherapy a shot. Most come in with the "I've nothing to lose by experiencing this" attitude. Others have tested out all kinds of different modalities, and then finally resorted to receiving Hypnotherapy. I have had clients who came to me because somebody they respected and loved commented on the results they were having and referred them to me.

Why it Works!
Maureen Pisani Ph.D.
www.ProThriveSBH.com

Regardless of how they found me, they were each at least curious and open to see what results could be achieved. In 16 years, I had three clients who refused to collaborate.

In this survey, there was one client who said that they didn't receive any results, and another one who stated that they didn't realize that they needed to listen to the recording to continue strengthening the suggestions. I'm sharing these so you can see the full spectrum of results. Almost all the clients achieve the desired results, while 59.18% claimed that they received results that were surprising and outstanding.

Resultant outcomes through Hypnotherapy are not only determined by how acceptable the suggestions are, but how the dynamics of the clients' surroundings are. There have been scenarios when the clients did accept the suggestions, but upon implementing the new behaviors, their upgraded behavior tipped the family dynamics in such a way that the family rebelled against, sabotaged, or judged the client negatively. When that happens, the clients revert to the old behavior to keep the peace and maintain the established family dynamics, even though they are aware that it's contrary to their desired goals.

Why it Works!
Maureen Pisani Ph.D.
www.ProThriveSBH.com

235

I have had countless clients who, in spite of my telling them verbally and the instructions I send in the email with the recording, have never listened to it again, and yet, the upgrade was accepted and implemented. I send the recording to the clients so that they have (i) full ownership and (ii) full access to it. I share with the clients that I believe in empowering them, so should they ever face a similar situation, their first recourse is to re-listen to the recording and yes, it will re-trigger their desired behaviors and outcomes once again.

In all my years in practice, I have seen clients who were mildly interested in gaining the results, and others who were beyond determined to do their best in session with me, so as to receive the absolute best results. I have seen clients who dealt with minor situations like it was the end of the world for them, and others who dealt with horrific tragedies like it was just a broken fingernail.

I have observed, guided, and served thousands of clients and each has taught me something - especially the realization to never assume. I ask questions to ensure that understanding, comprehension, and intentions are clear between me and the client. It is truly essential for the best outcome possible.

Yes, I work within what's in scope of the Hypnotherapy boundaries, but I also come from the perspective that

Why it Works!
Maureen Pisani Ph.D.
www.ProThriveSBH.com

Hypnotherapy has, can, and might work for whatever the clients' presenting complaints are. Being that I have extensive medical training, thanks to having been an X-ray technician in Malta for nine years, I utilize all that knowledge to serve my clients in aspects of life that most hypnotherapists don't. Plus, I'm living proof that Hypnotherapy can resolve incredibly painful and bewildering health conditions, so I very rarely decline a client. I am always candid, blunt, and honest. I explain to them the medical part, then the hypnotic approach, and then when they agree, they've basically authorized me to help them overcome their health issue, be it acute or chronic. It is an incredible honor to watch the clients experience this outstanding results.

Why it Works!
Maureen Pisani Ph.D.
www.ProThriveSBH.com

237

CHAPTER 9

PERSONAL OBSERVATIONS

Research that studies peoples and/or groups of people are known as "Ethnographies." They entail getting immersed in the culture, experiencing life with the people one is studying, recording observations, and then stating what the observations were.

I decided to go a step further than just writing an Ethnography. Yes, I immersed myself in the culture – a segment of humanity, specifically a group of people who are aware that something's not quite right in their life and they are ready, willing, and open to face it, fix it and live the benefits.

I met with these people on a regular basis for a decent amount of time. Currently, I can say that I've been hypnotizing people for 16 years, as I plan on hypnotizing people for the rest of my life. Some clients I have had the honor of working with consistently for years. Others sought me for hypnotherapy, resolved their issue, and discontinued the sessions, only to return to me to resolve other issues.

Why it Works!
Maureen Pisani Ph.D.
www.ProThriveSBH.com

Having these clients return to me for subsequent upgrades not only confirms the efficacy of hypnotherapy, but also reinforces their trust in me, and for that I'm beyond honored. Other clients have had sessions with me to tackle one topic and only one topic. For over more than a decade and a half, it has been my absolute pleasure to watch these people transform and blossom into incredible beings enjoying successfully upgraded lives.

It always makes me chuckle when a client reaches out to me after a while and feels the need to remind me who they are. I know they are aware that I have worked with thousands of people, so their reminding me is appreciated. What they don't realize that I have them "filed" in the recesses of my mind. So as soon as they start talking, describing their life, something they do or say will instantly trigger my memory and I know exactly who they are. These clients are always surprised when I share with them how I remember them. The secret is that when I'm in session, I give my clients undivided attention. I'm focused on them, listening, writing notes, and planning their hypnotic suggestions. This level of focus results in having them etched into my memory. I have dedicated my life to serving my clients at my best, so they in turn can experience their best life possible.

Why it Works!
Maureen Pisani Ph.D.
www.ProThriveSBH.com

239

Having been blessed with so many clients, I am able to extract what the norms are, what works and what doesn't, what causes resistance, where the resistance is, how to overcome it, and how to help the clients take one step at a time where they gift themselves a better future.

I have always believed that clients deserved successful outcomes. They came to me for a reason. They were trusting me and my expertise to help them, support them, teach them, and guide them through dealing with and resolving the issue(s) that they were facing. I have intentionally always gone above and beyond what was expected of me, because I believe that each of my clients deserves my best. I have done that, I am doing that, and I will continue to do that regardless of what the norms are, regardless of what anyone else does, because ultimately that's what integrity is to me…doing one's best at all times.

SELF-IDENTITY. As I went through the years, I started noticing how impactful our Self-Identity was. It wasn't something that had been brought up in any of my previous studies.

Why it Works!
Maureen Pisani Ph.D.
www.ProThriveSBH.com

We are all aware of Self-Confidence and Self-Esteem, but not the others. However, all six affect each and every thought, decision, and subsequent action. Understanding these self-identity attributes and working them into my sessions created results.

I started by testing out the waters. I asked people with autoimmune diseases (where one's own cells attack one's own body) hard questions like *"What needs to happen for you to love you more?"* The shock that showed up on the clients' faces was proof as to how unexpected the question was for them. However, the shock was always followed by tears. Men and women broke down, commenting on how I went straight to the heart of things. I believe in creating results, so asking the hard questions was bringing up the truth, which is what the client needed to face to be able to process it, resolve it and release it to overcome the hurdle they were dealing with.

When I would ask *"what needs to happen..."* I asked it this way on purpose. I didn't ask *"What do you need to do?"* because that would imply that they had failed themselves.

Why it Works!
Maureen Pisani Ph.D.
www.ProThriveSBH.com

241

I asked *"What needs to happen..."* because it offers the possibility that things are going improve from this point forward. Regretting the past is wasted energy. All we can do is assess and acknowledge the current situation, and work on creating a better now that will lead to a better future. After asking, I wait. I never assume that the client cannot come up with what they think needs to happen to prove to themselves that they love themselves.

Usually, they can give examples of what they can do to love themselves more. If after I ask, there's a prolonged silence, then and only then will I suggest some things, which inevitably prompts the client to start sharing what is within their capability to implement.

Over time, I noticed that when the self-identity attributes were strong, we hardly ever brought them up. It was only when the levels were low that introducing these traits was beneficial and enlightening to the clients. When people were in crisis and hard decisions needed to be made, I guided them through seeing the same scenarios through different points of view, highlighting the advantages and disadvantages of each perspective.

Why it Works!
Maureen Pisani Ph.D.
www.ProThriveSBH.com

SURVIVAL MECHANISMS. As I worked with the same clients over prolonged periods of time, I saw patterns of behaviors where stressors would trigger the clients' survival mechanisms. I observed and learned how each of the clients was wired. It was enlightening to realize how to guide the clients into achieving their goals without triggering their survival mechanisms. Observing their reactions, as I walked them through step by step how they could survive their worst-case scenarios, was exhilarating.

They had been functioning from that instinctive primary assessment that anything stressful had the potential to kill them. I would explain that as children, when we were afraid of monsters, the monsters only had power over us until we looked. Once we saw that there was nothing to be afraid of, the monsters lost all their power. So, I walked them through facing the absolute worst scenario they could imagine. As soon as they described it, I asked, *"And then what would happen?"* and they'd go down a level deeper into what they imagined would be the next terrifying, potentially life-threatening experience. As soon as they finished describing it, I would keep asking *"And then what would happen?"* At some point the clients would look up at me and say *"Nothing?"* or *"That's it?"* or *"I guess I'd be ok,"* to which I'd answer *"Precisely! You would survive!"*

Why it Works!
Maureen Pisani Ph.D.
www.ProThriveSBH.com

243

The reason I walked them through this exercise is because my telling them that they would survive it wouldn't have had any impact. There had been several people in these clients' lives that had told them that already. My intention was to have the clients imagine the terrifying experience, which would trigger their sympathetic nervous system, while in a safe space – my office.

Then I would take them down gradually, at their own pace. This allowed them, their conscious mind, their unconscious mind, and their primitive mind to work through every possible nuance of the situation. When they themselves ran out of horrible scenarios and realized that they would survive it, because they themselves realized it, the realization was beyond acceptable and was accepted. It was irrefutable because their own wiring had come up with it! This would result in a dissolution of the monster (their worst-case scenario) and the breakthrough of the realization that they can handle life and that yes, they will survive any case scenario!

Explaining the five survival mechanisms was on a need-to-know basis. I only shared information regarding a particular survival mechanism if it was pertinent to the client's resolving their presenting complaint.

Why it Works!
Maureen Pisani Ph.D.
www.ProThriveSBH.com

Most knew of Fight and Flight, less knew about Freeze, and almost none knew about Food and *The Other F.*

Introducing these survival mechanisms to clients was always enlightening to them. It explained why they did what they did in a nonjudgmental way. It explained why they felt such a drive to behave that way. As humans, people always need to understand what happened to them and why it happened.

Things need to make sense, especially if it's their own behavior. When individuals behave in a way that to them is irrational, inappropriate, scandalous, or outrageous, it shocks them, and sometimes the negative self-judgment can do more damage that the actual stressful/traumatic incident.

I know of a case when a woman severely injured her back and went to the Emergency Room. After the tests were completed, the ER physician informed her that she had herniated three discs in her lower back. She sat there, nodding in what seemed like agreement and acceptance.

Why it Works!
Maureen Pisani Ph.D.
www.ProThriveSBH.com

245

She received all the treatment orders and on leaving the hospital, went directly to a bakery and ordered a lemon-flavored, jelly-filled donut! She later confessed that as soon as the ER doctor said the words "three herniated discs" she stopped listening to him and could only think of where the nearest bakery was. She explained that she felt like it was beyond her control to go anywhere else than to that bakery first, even before stopping at the pharmacy to pick up her prescriptions! She felt that her reaction was absurd and outrageous and couldn't understand why anyone would react that way.

I explained that apparently, she had an unconscious "severity" threshold of what she considered "manageable" as opposed to "serious," and the phrase "three herniated discs" tipped her situation into "serious," to the point of triggering her survival mechanism - Food. Only when she had satisfied that instinctive request was, she able to continue functioning from her conscious mind. Understanding what happened helped her realize that her behavior, albeit unexpected, was truly quite within normal human behavior. It also eased the negative self-judgment and self-criticism.

Why it Works!
Maureen Pisani Ph.D.
www.ProThriveSBH.com

As a therapist, bound by confidentiality, I'm honored with the clients' uncensored experiences. I'm truly humbled that my life's mission is to help and soothe those in pain. When they unburden their souls with what they think are horrible behaviors, these people are terrified of being judged. Instead, I offer them an explanation that's beyond proven in science, explaining that how they behaved was just their most primitive triggers going into action in a desperate effort to keep them safe and alive.

When I explain to these people why they chose to have sex when a tragedy had just occurred, in this way, there's instant relief, instant self-forgiveness, and instant understanding. Yes, I do teach them how to recognize what the stressors are, when to implement a "Pause" so they can take a moment to assess, think, and respond accordingly. My reasoning, which I explain to the clients, is that should they face a serious stressor that might trigger *The Other F* again, instead of being reactive, knowing that they might regret the action afterwards, introducing the assessing techniques offers them the opportunity to choose to be proactive, to choose to function from their conscious mind, to choose to function from their pre-frontal cortices instead of having that prehistoric knee jerk reaction.

Why it Works!
Maureen Pisani Ph.D.
www.ProThriveSBH.com

247

HIGH LEVELS VS. LOW LEVELS. I have also found that people who have high self-identity levels function from a completely different perspective than other individuals who have low levels. The people with the high levels know where they stand, what their capabilities are, what's acceptable and what isn't, what they deserve and what they're worth; and because of how much they love themselves will adhere to certain behaviors and maintain a positive lifestyle.

However, the individuals who have low levels of self-identity attributes, tend to have shorter positive times and longer miserable times. This happens primarily because they are not sure if they are worthy or deserving of being treated right.

They do, however, have incredible amounts of compassion, understanding, forgiveness, and love for everyone else other than themselves. Internally, they do have their "wish list" of standards, but in the moment of truth, they succumb to the others' negative behavior.

Here's how they prolong the miserable times and negative behavior.

Just for the sake of argument, let's say that Jill is in a relationship with Jack.

Why it Works!
Maureen Pisani Ph.D.
www.ProThriveSBH.com

Now, Jill has her comfort zone of what she knows is proper behavior. Yes, it's internal but she knows it's there. Jack says/does something that's a little off – it's not really appropriate, but it's also not totally outrageous. It bothers Jill, but she doesn't do or say anything. Jack is aware that he crossed a line or two, but he is also aware that Jill didn't react negatively, which makes him feel emboldened, and so finds another occasion to do/say something more inappropriate! Now, he's gone to nearly the very extreme of Jill's comfort zone of behavior, but Jill still doesn't respond or react. Jill rationalizes that Jack isn't aware of what he's doing – it was just a mistake, he was drunk, he was uncomfortable amongst her friends, he was tired/stressed, his sports team had just lost, he had just been fired from his job, he was… he was… he was….

Jill will continue to find excuses to minimize how Jack's behavior is seen by others. Internally, she's beyond hurt, but she's forgiving, understanding, and truly cannot conceive how Jack could possibly do that intentionally, so she allows her comfort zone to extend to accommodate Jack's behavior. Jack is amazed that Jill swept that incident under the rug and is now on a mission to see how far he can push the envelope.

Why it Works!
Maureen Pisani Ph.D.
www.ProThriveSBH.com

249

Jack's negative behavior continues to intensify, and with each insult, with each betrayal, Jill keeps extending and extending her comfort zone to what she deems "acceptable," becoming less and less positive, and in actuality, becomes incredibly negative and abusive. This goes on until Jack does something unthinkable, something so extreme, that only then can Jill recognize how bad his behavior is. Only then will she draw the line where enough is enough. However, by then, she's been beaten down, invalidated, taken for granted, abused, cheated on, lied to, and stolen from, that what's left is only a shadow of who Jill used to be.

Yes, please keep in mind that Jill could do exactly the same thing to Jack. I just chose one scenario to make the explanation easier.

When I explain this vicious abusive cycle to the clients, they are shocked, horrified, and mortified. Most of them have sought me out after most of this cycle has already occurred. They are beyond stupefied that their partner's behavior is intentional. They are shocked that I know what they've gone through and how this chapter in their life is going to end. Each of these clients honestly thinks that they're the only ones to whom this is happening.

Why it Works!
Maureen Pisani Ph.D.
www.ProThriveSBH.com

They have kept it a secret because they honestly thought so little of themselves that they blamed themselves for the outcome they were living. As their therapist, I guide them through seeing their own worth, setting standards for themselves, setting boundaries on how others behave with them, finding their voice, helping them construct sentences and phrases that they are comfortable stating with strength. I help them find their own strength and build them up to the point where they know that their boundaries have to be respected, honored, and implemented by their partners. If, once they set safe, reasonable, appropriate boundaries, their partners continue abusing them, then they have full awareness that their partner's behavior is intentional, and breaking away becomes the appropriate thing to do.

FEAR VS SAFE. As I've mentioned before, as soon as people feel stressed, overwhelmed, or out of their depth, most realize that they are also afraid. This fear instantly enhances the clients' insecurities, and all they focus on is what they cannot do, what their weaknesses are, and how they are going to fail, lose, or even potentially die.

Why it Works!
Maureen Pisani Ph.D.
www.ProThriveSBH.com

251

Their fear is debilitating and keeps them stuck in the crisis and in crisis mode. They can consciously understand what needs to happen and what they need to do to remove themselves from that situation, but their fear is paralyzing, and these people are unable to do what is otherwise seen as beyond safe to implement.

As their therapist, the first thing to do is start building a foundation where they realize, recognize, and feel that they are safe. This is probably the slowest portion of their journey. Helping these individuals realize their strengths is the first step of many upgrades. Having them role play what they are going to say to different people gets their mind comfortable with the words and phrases, and they feel better knowing that they are prepared.

I help them prepare themselves for all potential outcomes. The more they plan, the more we reduce potential unknowns. Anxiety and fear fester in what the clients consider unknown scenarios. When I bring up unforeseen events and walk the clients through different scenarios, just discussing all the pros and cons of these situations helps the clients build a library of possible situations, responses, and outcomes. The more prepared the clients are, the stronger they feel, and the closer to a breakthrough they are.

Why it Works!
Maureen Pisani Ph.D.
www.ProThriveSBH.com

I help them pre-plan what to do once they achieve their breakthrough. I guide them through realizing how capable they are, how resourceful they are, and how resilient they are, by looking back at everything they've already overcome.

I explain it this way. Think of how freeways are built. Initially there's a wooden structure, then a network of rebar is placed, then the concrete is poured into the wooden framework. But even after all these steps have been done, it's appropriate and wise to wait, as the concrete is given time to solidify. Only when that time is over, and the concrete has been determined to be completely cured and therefore solid, is the wooden frame removed. Only after it's been tested is the freeway open to traffic. This gives the clients internal permission to give themselves time to prepare, plan, and wait for the right time to execute their plans or new behavior.

THE NEED TO BELONG. Another behavior that I observed that was significant in a lot of clients was that their internal need to belong overrode most all of their pre-determined standards. I appreciate that our need to belong, from an evolutionary standpoint, has helped us survive.

Why it Works!
Maureen Pisani Ph.D.
www.ProThriveSBH.com

253

I know that from around 6 months of age, babies recognize that Mom is their lifeline (for both nourishment and care), and that she is a different entity then they are, so that's why babies of that age become "fussy." They are aware that if Mom isn't around, their food source isn't around and that could lead to their death. Yes, six-month-old babies have that innate knowing. It's an epigenetic inheritance that has travelled down the generations. Remember that traits that helped to ensure the survival of the species were reinforced as they were passed down through our ancestors.

That need to belong is seen in how children congregate with their siblings or classmates; how teenagers go through their phases to belong to this group or the other. We even notice it with adults, whether it's how they support their sports team, political party, and even their religious affiliation. Belonging is an absolute necessity, because deep down in each of our cells, there's that resonating knowing that belonging means surviving, and we're a species that will do everything and anything to survive.

As good and as essential as belonging is, however, there are situations and scenarios we're holding onto that belonging is detrimental to people.

Why it Works!
Maureen Pisani Ph.D.
www.ProThriveSBH.com

I observed countless clients who were in abusive relationships. When I use the word "abusive," I don't only mean physical abuse, which is when the partner raises their hand and strikes the person. There are all kinds of abuse: verbal abuse, when the supposedly loving partner says horrendous things to the other person with the intention to break them down, belittle them, humiliate them, manipulate them, and more. There's also emotional abuse, where the partner withholds positive emotion and instead ignores, invalidates, ridicules, and does spiteful and hurtful things to the individual. There's also mental abuse, where the partner intentionally lies, says things to gaslight the other person, instigates them to no end so the other person is constantly on edge, or creates scenarios where the partner has orchestrated the entire thing simply to get the person to doubt themselves. There's sexual abuse, where the partner either withholds sex from the person and intentionally flaunts that they are sexually active with someone else or knows where the person's boundaries are and attempts to (and sometimes succeeds) force them into sexual activities that are unacceptable to that person, but the partner claims the infamous sentence,

Why it Works!
Maureen Pisani Ph.D.
www.ProThriveSBH.com

255

"IF you really loved me, you'd do that for me." Then if the person refuses, the partner will reject that person because they didn't participate; but if the person surrenders and participates, then the partner will call them horrible names, intensifying the degradation. This is a downward spiraling vicious cycle.

Anything that any person forces someone else to do, behave, think, or feel IS ABUSE. AND... IT IS ALWAYS WRONG. There is no excusing or rationalizing abuse. It is wrong...period.

Then a problem arise when the partner is abusive and the other person, my client, has a desperate need to belong, and so rationalizes and excuses everything and anything that the abusive partner does. It is truly heartbreaking for me to witness this.

This is where I have had to walk a very fine line, and choose my words very carefully, because although my ultimate goal is to get the client to live and experience a better life, if I ever said that they should break up or leave their partner, I knew that their deep need to belong would have them reject my advice and choose their partner.

I had a client who was head over heels in love with his partner and would have done anything for her.

Why it Works!
Maureen Pisani Ph.D.
www.ProThriveSBH.com

She, however, was more attentive to her dog. She catered to her dog to the extent that her life revolved around the dog's schedule. On some level, my client realized that his partner's obsession with her dog wasn't appropriate, but his need to belong overrode everything and anything. After years of dating, she had still set dates according to what was happening with her dog, and if they went for weekend trips, they had to stay at hotels that accepted dogs. Their weekend getaway activities (yes, even sex) were scheduled before or after the dog's 2-hour walks, because the dog's needs came first.

As much as I had heard of situations and conditions that clients had acquiesced to for the sake of being in a relationship, being relegated lower than a dog was a little too much in my opinion. I knew I was walking on thin ice, but I honestly couldn't not say it. The client shook his head, sighing, but didn't voice his response. I advised him that agreeing to have the dog with them on their getaways was one thing, but to have to wait for the dog to have its walk before even considering their together time was truly unacceptable. He commented on the fact that he too thought that that was a little too extreme. We worked on what to say and how to say it. However, it seems that his need to belong to that relationship outweighed his self-identity attributes, because I never heard from him again.

Why it Works!
Maureen Pisani Ph.D.
www.ProThriveSBH.com

257

It is truly heartbreaking for me to watch how some people treat their supposed romantic interests with degradation and humiliation, and how painful it must be for these individuals who recognize what the behavior is, but simply cannot even consider leaving that abusive setting. Their need to belong and the terror they feel at the thought of walking away is just too much for them. These people only see how they won't belong with that one person. They never consider that once they disconnect from that abusive partner, they might connect, experience, and possibly receive true love from someone else. It's not even on their horizon that they might satisfy that need to belong with someone else. That's one of the reasons people who are in abusive relationships take so long to leave, because they're petrified that they will remain alone for the rest of their lives and never belong with anyone else.

This feeling of being locked in is compounded when the abusive relationship is in the family of origin. When these individuals are being abused by people in their family, in their inner circle, the betrayal is compounded because the person being abused is absolutely correct in doubting if they will ever be able to find another group of people with whom they can belong. Plus, they also have the shame, blame, and guilt of even considering breaking away from the family.

Why it Works!
Maureen Pisani Ph.D.
www.ProThriveSBH.com

Most cultures regard the family and its members as sacrosanct, but we know that family members do abuse other family members. So, when the person is being attacked, and considers breaking away from the source of the abuse, they are instantly overwhelmed with what everyone else is going to think of them and how they are going to be judged, which intensifies the severity of their potential decision.

The situation must worsen tremendously, and the person being abused must have incredible strength to finally break free, stand up for themselves, speak their truth, and choose to live their lives where respect is mandatory. Regardless of which situation they find themselves in, RESPECT is essential for anything else to be present. Without respect there can be no integrity, ethics, or love. Abusers have no respect for the people they attack. So, when these individuals demand to be respected, if other people agree to and do respect them, then there is a foundation for other positive attributes to be built and created. However, if the basic need for respect isn't honored, then nothing else survives.

Why it Works!
Maureen Pisani Ph.D.
www.ProThriveSBH.com

259

AUTHENTICITY AND INTEGRITY. Countless times I have stated to clients that I would never give them advice I wouldn't follow or implement myself. This standard has proven to be quite effective, because it strengthened my authenticity and subsequently my advice. I remember during a session, where I was advising a client on taking a stand, the client looked me straight in the eye and asked me, "Would you do that?" To which I responded without blinking an eye, "Yes, I have." The look on the client's face was priceless. In this world nowadays, when people have a relaxed relationship with the truth, and ethics and integrity are rare commodities, I pride myself on being a stickler and honoring myself and each of my clients by being ethical, honorable, and in integrity.

I have shared innumerable times that a straight line is a straight line and only a straight line. What I mean by that is that if I claim to be in integrity, there can be no bending of the rules, because then my line in the sand, which I claim to be a straight line, will no longer be straight. Fair? The only way I know how to not cross the ethical line is to never get close to it. I know what's right and what's wrong. Considering that I find myself as the therapist clients look up to for guidance, I hold myself to the highest of standards, for their sake as well as mine.

Why it Works!
Maureen Pisani Ph.D.
www.ProThriveSBH.com

I find it incongruous to be guiding a client in eating clean where their nutrition is sugar and wheat free, while I'm eating wheat and sugar regularly. So, for me to be in a position where I'm advising my clients on how to live a good life, it's incumbent upon me to already be walking my talk. Fair?

I find it to be the epitome of hypocrisy if I'm advising clients not to cheat on their partners if I'm having an affair, right? My private life, yes, is private, but if a client asks me point blank on what I've done in my life, how I've lived my personal life and made personal decisions, I do tell the truth. The uncensored truth. In those moments, I share with clients that if they called me in 20 years and asked me the same question, they would get the same answer, because the truth is the truth. There are no versions of the truth.

Nowadays, unfortunately, a large percentage of the population tends to think that saying something is the same as doing it. There are a couple of quotes that I'd like to share here:

(1) *"What you say isn't who you are. What you do is who you are."* Carl Jung, and (2) that adage *"What people say is who they wish they are and what people do is who they truly are."*

Why it Works!
Maureen Pisani Ph.D.
www.ProThriveSBH.com

261

There's a part of the brain, the "Insula," that functions on expectation. Most people, just saying that at some point they might do this, or they might go there someday, has them feeling so good that it's as if they've achieved it already. This unfortunately creates people who live most of their lives promising themselves a lot and never achieving much. Just keep this in mind – *"Someday is a day of the weak."*

I've seen how these empty promises hurt everyone – the people who say them and the people they say them to. So, when I find myself in the therapist's role, I guarantee to each of my clients that if I say I'm going to do something, they can rest assured that it will be done. I keep that standard in every aspect of my life. That's the only way that the clients can feel safe, because they realize that they are.

Why it Works!
Maureen Pisani Ph.D.
www.ProThriveSBH.com

CHAPTER 10

CONCLUSION

As I look back on my journey as a hypnotherapist, I am in awe of how resilient humanity truly is. As a species, we go through so much, it's incredible. I have been gifted a front row seat as a Hypnotherapist, to observe people's wounds, their pain, their losses. I have walked by their side through these valleys, helping, guiding, and serving to the best of my capability.

It has been an eye-opening and awe-inspiring experience to watch countless people break through the harshest of situations, break free from so much pain, and experience the liberation which led them to living peaceful, happy, successful, and abundant lives. It is truly exhilarating to watch them blossom into these versions of themselves, where they are living a reality that exceeds their wildest dreams.

It's thanks to these clients' unrelenting drive for better that I've been able to observe and become aware as to how all the different aspects of who these people truly are work in collaboration. It happens when their innate strengths and intentional upgrades cooperate to create synergistic results that were and still are beyond phenomenal!

Why it Works!
Maureen Pisani Ph.D.
www.ProThriveSBH.com

263

Thanks to how they each progressed on their journey, I was able to continuously personalize what I said, and how I said it, both cognitively and hypnotically, to keep them moving forward. As the adjustments and upgrades were received and implemented, continued success was achieved and experienced.

Becoming aware of how the self-identity attributes interacted and affected their survival mechanisms helped me serve, guide, and lead my clients to a better future. Teaching them what the attributes were, and sharing information that helped them understand their behavior without judgment, created the best possible environment. These people learned to fully release behaviors that didn't serve any longer. They also found that learning about, accepting, and implementing new positive behaviors with full ease and comfort was also possible.

The results were received, accepted, and implemented faster because through the Hypnotherapy modality, I was engaging the larger part of their mental capacity. Having their unconscious mind (88-97%) be on board, understand what the goal was, realize that it was safe, and have it support the conscious mind's goals, was truly the ultimate of collaborations.

Why it Works!
Maureen Pisani Ph.D.
www.ProThriveSBH.com

It is my ultimate goal to share all the benefits that Hypnotherapy offers, globally. Considering that everything we ingest, especially prescriptions, have all kinds of horrifying side effects, knowing that Hypnotherapy's only side effect is RELAXATION truly makes this modality not only beyond efficient and effective, but also one of the safest modalities to utilize.

Why it Works!
Maureen Pisani Ph.D.
www.ProThriveSBH.com

265

Biography

Maureen Pisani, Ph.D. is an international speaker, hypnotherapist, and best-selling author. She is the founder of Pro Thrive Science Based Hypnotherapy, where she works with individuals and groups (both in-person and online) to help empower them, streamline success, and truly thrive.

Aside from having a Ph.D. in Hypnotherapy, she is also a Trainer in Neuro-Linguistic Programming (NLP) and is at the Mastery Level in Therapeutic Guided Imagery, Emotional Freedom Technique (EFT Tapping), and Reiki energy work. She employs a variety of modalities when working with her clients to bring them the best tools and resources for positive and lasting change.

Maureen has also been a Director, Instructor, and Mentor at two nationally accredited universities where she shared her love and knowledge of Hypnotherapy. She was the Resident Hypnotherapist at the Chopra Center (Carlsbad, CA) for almost 9 years, until its closure in December 2019.

As of December 2021, she has published 18 books, including 3 best sellers. Maureen has also co-authored a research paper published by the Neuroscience Department at UCLA.

Maureen Pisani is the poster child for how hypnotherapy can help change your life for the better. After a work injury left her in constant pain and 100% disabled, she found that hypnotherapy offered her relief and a new lease on life. Although she now lives in Santa Fe, NM, Maureen is originally from the Island of Malta, and continues to share her love of her home country with all those she encounters. If you're interested in hypnotherapy – whether for events, virtual presentations, group or individual sessions, please contact Maureen and she'll be happy to answer your questions.

Why it Works!
Maureen Pisani Ph.D.
www.ProThriveSBH.com

267

Books

All products are available on www.ProThriveSBH.com and maureenpisani.com

- **Dare to Ask**
- **Against All Odds**
- **Invisible to Invincible**
- **'Timeless Hypnotic Scripts I'**
- **'Timeless Hypnotic Scripts II'**
- **'401 Study Guide'**
  - Supplementary Textbook to HMI 401 Course
- **3 Easy Steps to achieve *SUCCESS***
  - Hypnotherapy & EFT Workbook with 3 Hypnotic MP3s
- **3 Easy Steps for *Relationships***
  - Hypnotherapy & EFT Workbook with 3 Hypnotic MP3s
- **3 Easy Steps for *Weight Management***
  - Hypnotherapy & EFT Workbook with 3 Hypnotic MP3s
- **3 Easy Steps for a successful *'Hypnotherapy Practice'***
  - Hypnotherapy & EFT Workbook with 3 Hypnotic MP3s

- **3 Easy Steps for *Resilience***
  - o Hypnotherapy & EFT Workbook with 1 Hypnotic MP3
- **Living a Pain & Medication Free Life**
  - o Hypnotherapy & EFT Workbook with 1 Hypnotic MP3
- **R.I.D. Relieving Intestinal Discomfort**
  - o Hypnotherapy & EFT Workbook with 1 Hypnotic MP3
- **Reducing Anxiety**
  - o Hypnotherapy & EFT Workbook with 1 Hypnotic MP3.
- **Conquering Crisis**
  - o Hypnotherapy & EFT Workbook with 1 Hypnotic MP3
- **Getting Away With It**

Why it Works!
Maureen Pisani Ph.D.
www.ProThriveSBH.com

269

Hypnotic MP3s:

Maureen has also produced the following MP3s.

- Power Nap
- Sleep Improvement
- Self-Confidence & Motivation
- Speaking up for yourself
- Reduction /Removal of Test Anxiety
- Enhanced Memory
- Achieving Success (3-disc set)
  - o Persistence
  - o Versatility
  - o Going for it!
- Weight Management (3-disc set)
  - o Transformation
  - o Permission to Change
  - o Acknowledging Success
- Relationships (3-MP3 set)
  - o Letting go of the Past
  - o Putting it all in place
  - o Drawing in the Right Relationship
- Pain Management (3-MP3 set)
  - o Sensitivity to Pain
  - o Healing Ability
  - o The 'in-between' space

Why it Works!
Maureen Pisani Ph.D.
www.ProThriveSBH.com

- Improving Health Conditions

- Improving Hair Conditions

- Improving Skin Condition

All products are available on www.prothrivesbh.com and maureenpisani.com

Why it Works!
Maureen Pisani Ph.D.
www.ProThriveSBH.com

271

TESTIMONIALS

The following are testimonials that were given in the survey that I sent out. The survey was set so that all responses were anonymous.

- "Ms. Pisani was recommended to me as I was new to the area and wanted to stop smoking. I had one session with Ms. Pisani, and I have not smoked since. Love her and would highly recommend. I had instant results!"

- "You have to be a Master at it! It has to be your TRUE calling. That is Maureen in a nutshell."

- "Maureen was the hypnotherapist at the Chopra Center when I did a week-long retreat with them. She did a great general session about hypnotherapy, and I decided to give it a try. And I'm glad I did."

- "Hypnotherapy takes little time and does require return visits. One session had me complete on issues I had carried for many years. As opposed to me being in counselling sessions for months or years to deal with the same issue(s). The related trauma of the past issues are not frightening and therefore can be dealt with in one session.

Why it Works!
Maureen Pisani Ph.D.
www.ProThriveSBH.com

Maureen's session was made available at a retreat. She was most effective, and I continued to see other appointments on other concerns I had about my stress causing issues. Relaxation with Maureen is quick and easy, and I have come to trust her completely. Maureen offers non-face-to-face opportunities to meet with her, which is awesome."

- "I liked the fact that Hypnotherapy is a non-pharmaceutical approach to pain relief I was first introduced to Maureen Pisani in a zoom format offered by Camp Chesterfield Spiritualist camp."

- "Life changing. I sought help to improve my personal relationship, to boost my sales team performance and to treat my PTSD. All were successfully treated and I still have the benefits of those treatments today."

- "Hypnotherapy works! One of my sessions helped me sleep better and have more clarity when I worked. My mind was clearer and sharper. Maureen is truly the best. She listens and cares about what you're going through. She asks all the right questions to then create the perfect recording for you. I try to listen to her recordings every (day) and on the days I don't, I definitely feel a difference since things don't go as smoothly. She is a remarkable woman and an expert in her craft. I have also sent friends to her and she's also done wonders for them."

Why it Works!
Maureen Pisani Ph.D.
www.ProThriveSBH.com

273

- "The most impactful experiences I have had in my quest for healing and revelation. Maureen was referred to me by a trusted friend."

- "Maureen was my favorite instructor at the Hypnosis Motivation Institute. I felt a very strong rapport with her. During my first session Maureen was friendly, attentive, patient and knowledgeable. She listened intently to everything I said. I was amazed that a 40-year stress problem that I had tried to rectify on my own was resolved in one session. And the change has maintained for the past 13 years. I would recommend Maureen to anyone considering hypnotherapy."

- "Her credentials were outstanding and her commitment to provide service is unprecedented. She's committed to her participants to achieve their goals."

- "I love the relaxed feeling that I get during the session and that listening to the recording integrates well into my nighttime routine. Maureen's voice is soothing and relaxing. I chose Maureen because she came highly recommended, and I am glad I did! She is an expert in her field and gets results!"

- "Maureen came highly recommended by a family member who had great success. She put my mother at great ease and she said she felt amazing afterwards. When I play the recording, my mom always says how great she feels."

Why it Works!
Maureen Pisani Ph.D.
www.ProThriveSBH.com

- "I loved that it took virtually no effort and made such a big change for me. I also loved that it instantly helped me sleep. Instead of my negative thoughts running through my mind, I had Maureen's beautiful affirmations running through my mind all day. It made all the difference."

- "There are a few people that I would trust with altering the connections in my brain. Maureen is one of them. She listens intently and personalizes every session. She helped me finish my PhD, and I continue to turn to her for guidance. If you have found her – then you are lucky."

- "It's not about liking hypnotherapy, per se, it's about the compassion, understanding, professionalism, psychic ability, and ability and skill of Maureen. Had not considered "hypno" as the method of therapy until suggested and referred by a close friend."

- "I like the techniques you taught for getting out of a sympathetic state. I still use those today when I get overwhelmed with stress. I like the meditative state I was put in during the session. I like that I received a recording that I can use when I'm working to clear stress and trauma.

Why it Works!
Maureen Pisani Ph.D.
www.ProThriveSBH.com

275

I chose to work with you during my Perfect Health Retreat at the Chopra Center. I was happy with my session. Though I did not continue to listen to the recording, I did get the benefits from the session. Hypnotherapy was one of many techniques I tried/learned in my journey to healing, and I'm glad I experienced it. I would definitely do it again."

- "Remarkable results for something that is inexpensive, non-invasive, and requires very little time and effort on my part. Maureen Pisani came highly recommended, and I really like her energy and approach. Just one hour spent with Maureen and I no longer suffer from insomnia, and my anxiety level has decreased significantly. I am looking forward to conquering other issues with her guidance!"

Why it Works!
Maureen Pisani Ph.D.
www.ProThriveSBH.com

Why it Works!
Maureen Pisani Ph.D.
www.ProThriveSBH.com

277